GAE AULENTI

Margherita Petranzan

GAE AULENTI

SKIRA

Photos by Gae Aulenti at start of chapters
p. 16 : Exhibition by Peter Cripps in Melbourne, 1996
p. 80: The anechoic chamber at Nanking University, 1974
p. 138: The Great Wall of China, 1974
p. 198: Jantar Mantar in Delhi, 1971
p. 226: Singapore, 1972

On inside pages:
p. 200: Olivetti Showroom, Paris, 1967
p. 201: Apartment in Via Gesù, Milan, 1974
p. 202: House in San Michele di Pagana, Genoa, 1973
p. 203: Tivioli Showroom, Milan, 1996
pp. 240-241: 13th Milan Triennale, Italian section *Il Tempo delle Vacanze*, 1964

Volume edited by Milena Archetti (Studio Aulenti, Milan)

Editorial coordination: Caterina Giavotto
Translation: Lucinda Byatt (Edinburgh, UK)
Copyeditor: Michael Aneiro
Editing: Roberto Marro
Layout: Antonietta Pietrobon

First published in Italy in 2003 by
Rizzoli libri illustrati
Società Editoria Artistica SpA
Gruppo Skira
via Torino 61
20123 Milano
Italy
www.skira.net

Printed and bound in Italy. First edition.

ISBN: 88-8491-591-0

Distributed in UK by Thames and Hudson Ltd.,
181a High Holborn, London WC1V 7QX, United Kingdom.

CONTENTS

ORDER AND TRANSGRESSION

Words of stone
Introduction by Margherita Petranzan

"Is true criticism not as rare as art itself?"

Mies van der Rohe, 1930

"The artist must only serve himself, the architect society"

Adolf Loos, Spoken into the Void

This book presents the *opera omnia* of Gae Aulenti in an attempt to highlight her rigorous approach to every minute detail forming part of the design area.

Living in and on her projects day in and day out has slowly, almost naturally, organized her "life project" in complete symbiosis with her work. Gae Aulenti can certainly be said to view the "project" as life, and vice versa life becomes the project.

For an architect I believe it is vitally important to be able to "project oneself" by constantly applying constructive self-criticism to one's own actions. This leads to renovation, first and foremost of oneself, but also offers a chance to step outside that inexact dimension of the immediacy of vision, which is normally regarded as an objective fact on which every project is based, because, as Valéry says, "observing almost always means imagining what you expect to see," given that man lives and moves inside what he sees, but he only sees what he thinks. Starting with the awareness that thought and vision often lead to stagnation in either the past or the future, because they overlook or neglect the pure instant, that essential and decisive moment for the project, because nothing is perhaps more abstract than the vision of the present as it is: *nothing is more abstract than what exists.*

I have entitled this introduction dedicated to her works *Words of Stone* because it amply expresses the poetics of her work, organized with obstinacy and determination and rooted in the "ancient sign language" that architecture has always contained and still embodies, even in its most daring and provocative innovations.

On the one hand, the title conjures up Adolf Loos' *Spoken into the Void*, in which—attributing a fundamental value to the "word" freed from "ornaments"—he affirmed that only careful observation and accurate description could lead to an understanding, knowledge and identification of the architectural ob-

"Practicing architecture means beginning by creating for myself the greatest number of constraints possible, constraints that I take from the place itself as well as from the disciplines. In fact, one of the nicest compliments that anyone can give to an architectural work is to say that it seems that it has always existed in that context."

(all the quotations on these pages printed in italics are by Gae Aulenti)

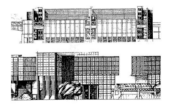

above: Bicocca project, Milan, 1986

left: Site for Musée d'Orsay, Paris, 1984

previous pages:
Set for King Lear by William Shakespeare. Directed by Luca Ronconi. Rome, Teatro Argentina and Milan, Teatro Lirico, 1995.

"I am convinced that architecture is connected to the polis, it is an art of the city, of the foundation, so it cannot help but refer to and be conditioned by that specific context in which it is born. The place, the time and the culture shape one architecture rather than another."

ject. On the other, it refers to the "Stone figures" of radical architecture (Archizoom and Superstudio) and a certain architectural avant-garde movement dating from the 1960s and 70s from which Gae Aulenti adopted the fiercely critical and prophetic attitude that hypothesized "aesthetic civilisations" and "total arts," while still feeling the need to recover the concept of "work" and its "semantic organic unity." Her approach is also "activated" by the artistic avant-garde movements which, in the pages of various magazines ("Casabella-Continuità," Vittorini's "Menabò," "Il Verri," "Quindici") questioned the functionality of language by overturning the results using the instrument of "rejection" and "transgression," and using the collage technique or the happening as habitual forms of representation. This led her to experiment with sophisticated new construction techniques, as well as new forms of architectural language.

Her architecture can be described as a sort of constant exercise in self-reflection, which calls for rigorous composition and the search for new technologies that slowly distance themselves from fashionable movements.

She stands out for her international style, which is essentially linked to a fortunate series of important commissions and competition awards that have allowed her to construct her works in different environmental and cultural realities. Her style overturns the principles of rigid symmetry in new organization systems for both spaces and forms, "condemning" all arbitrary decoration. This book aims to give the fullest possible scope to her internationalism and her capacity to provide answers that are, on the one hand, deeply rooted in the most severe and controlled language of architectural discipline, and on the other sensitive to the widely diverse situations and stimuli provided by places and their history.

I also chose the title "Words of stone" because stone, the material that *par excellence* is linked to architecture and is extraordinarily representative of its tectonic nature—its exact and necessary roots in the earth, which is mother and at the same time life—is both strong and living, giving solidity, variety of shape, and safety to every structure built.

Lastly, "Words of stone" is also apt because the language of architecture, which is similar to the spoken word, constructs the architectural phrase and consequently the complex fin-

Studies for rocking chair
Sgarsul, 1962

ished argument, the city, through its "words of stone," namely the buildings and the whole built environment.

Gae Aulenti's "words of stone" have methodically and firmly left the mark of her strongly eclectic and disenchanted work on the world, unconstrained by formal stylistic elements and stubbornly "realistic," strengthened by her conviction that we must exercise untiringly only the part of us that "chooses," the part that "implements."

Broadly speaking, the book is divided into three parts: the first is an introduction, because it intends to start—with all the difficulties entailed in any *beginning*—this presentation of a complex work and an "authoritative" personality, about whom any hasty enunciation will appear simplistic and inconsistent to say the least.

However, I can affirm that I was able to write about Gae Aulenti's works, and indeed I wanted to do so solely because I also design and build. I believe that only someone who has experienced the fiery enthusiasm and tremendous tension of every moment of ideation—someone who has conceived the project for an undertaking that they alone can abandon, someone who is subject to the scruple of inner objections, the struggle of alternative ideas that emerge in continuous antagonism seeking to gain supremacy, the need to ensure that the strongest and most universal ones always triumph over the most recent, someone who has been obliged to choose between thousands of directions that have then been abandoned, someone who has managed to see a non-existent building standing in thin air, someone who has suffered from the vertigo of seeing a goal retreat into the distance, from discouragement caused by the absent or slow progress of construction, someone who has experienced the richness, the resource and the spiritual space created by the conscious fact of building, and lastly someone who can imagine a whole covered by alterations, multiple qualities, infinite possible combinations, alternative materials and means—only someone like this can attempt to understand what a work of architecture represents.

However, this is a discrete departure, a prelude that anticipates the symphonic score to follow, which must have the necessary space to express its articulate composition. It is a departure based on words that attempt to connect the visible

"I believe that place is, first of all, a conceptual fact, a fact of culture. Indeed, if you work in Paris, Barcelona, Milan or Rome, the cultural conditions are different. Understanding and knowing these differences is necessary for anyone who undertakes design, necessary because one must constantly work with the tradition of a place."

traces, in the form of images, to the built objects, which as such are absent, like a fragile makeshift bridge spanning the void. But "words are also actions," affirmed Ludwig Wittgenstein in 1945, actions that build paths and structures, forge links, and evoke absences; actions that allow "relations."

The second part, the central, substantial part, shows the works, both built and unbuilt, through photos and drawings, divided into four chapters:

1. Roaming and Being Rooted

This chapter contains the works and projects that, on the one hand, show the international quality of the architect's work and her consequent capacity to understand and know the characteristics of the places where she is asked to work—in view of her propensity for travel. On the other hand, these projects convey her strong sense of being rooted to places that belong to her history and which, as a result, transmit values and emotions that are conveyed through the projects. It is worth noting that the attention paid to the location and her rigorous approach to analyzing all the components lead to different results on every occasion, namely results that are never standardized in line with empty formal stylistic elements.

2. Evocations

This chapter only contains unbuilt projects and competitions that express a strong sense of utopianism and experimentation and which evoke—in the sense of "bringing to light"—through isolation, the key components of the design operation. These are inserted in an evident poetic and intuitive tension.

Even the stage designs included in this chapter are not presented as simple installations, which normally take on a precarious appearance, but are instead seen as genuine architecture, complete with that more or less energetic but necessary abstraction and sense of construction used when building a work of architecture.

3. Order and Transgression

This chapter contains built projects and works that reveal the architect's eclecticism, her capacity to stretch design intuition as far as possible, turning it into a strongly transgressive sign, but at the same time underlining the importance in design of

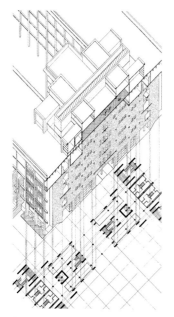

Re-use of Lingotto, Turin, international invited competition, 1983
Exploded axonometry

guaranteeing a rational compositional layout that is securely under absolute control, and never accidental.

4. Analogous Objects
The chapter focuses on design objects and comparative aspects of similar projects.

For Gae Aulenti, the study of working details is fundamentally important; it gives the measure of objects and relates them to the contexts in which they are used. A number of "dominant" themes within her designs, favorite areas that recur in several projects, emerge from these pages. Stairs, for example, are one such theme. Stairs are important because they help to perceive space inside a building, aside from the logic of distribution and perception based solely on planimetric parameters. This theme frequently appears in her designs as the "specious" search for signs that can transform the necessary structural connection between the various floors into an articulate and complex architectural product whose compositional autonomy gives it independent existence, in the same way as a statue.

The third and final part, which I have called COMMENTARIES – CORRESPONDENCE, consists of short aphoristic-type essays, organized around the major themes facing contemporary architecture, alternating with observations on specific projects by Gae Aulenti in epistolary form:
– Architecture and history;
– Architecture and politics;
– Architecture and technique;
– Architecture and art.

The commentaries are based on the presupposition and conviction that a critical analysis of architectural works is extraordinarily taxing, if not impossible, given that the real *opera* does not comprise the final form, but rather the series of approximations leading toward it, taking the form of a process rather than a "molded" form.

Furthermore, in the conviction that an architectural product cannot be separated from the period that has desired and allowed its construction, I believe it is necessary, or rather essential, to provide the coordinates of that epoch through an analysis of the "dominant traits" that characterize and condition the "identity" of built projects.

"The conscious principle of design is to produce forms that can create experience and at the same time can include individual experience with the serenity determined by an autonomous critical capacity."

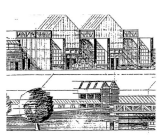

Entrance to Santa Maria Novella station, Florence, 1990
Studies to link the station to Pisa airport

ROAMING
AND
BEING ROOTED

House in the woods, 1963

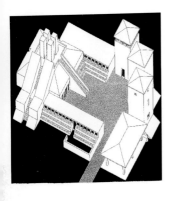

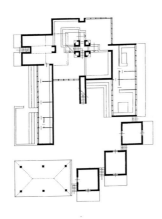

The villa includes the main house, three separate towers and a lean-to garage. The main structure comprises a living room, a mezzanine study, a dining room lit from above and two wings, one containing two bedrooms and bathrooms, and the other the kitchen and service rooms.

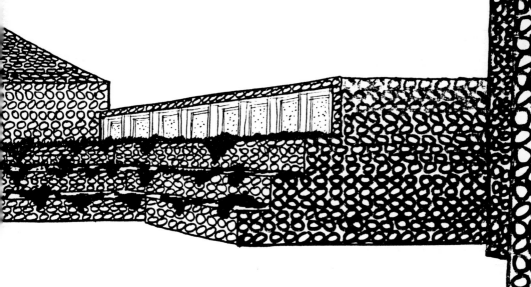

Garden in Tuscany, 1970

with Federico Zürcher

"I designed the Tuscan garden of Granaiolo in 1969 and each time I visit it or see it again in a photo, I am amazed that it exists. How could anyone, even intelligent individuals like my clients, have believed the drawings I submitted to the point that they decided to build it? How could anyone have imagined the metamorphosis from this strongly geometric design—hard and rational—to a natural harmony? Even for me, though I sensed the possibility, it was difficult to believe in the design. The idea was to follow the principle of land art, an art that penetrates the earth, that impresses an expression on the earth—without negating the long tradition of the *giardino all'italiana.*"

House in Pisa, 1973

with Federico Zürcher

Standing on the outskirts of Pisa in a housing development area, this house consists of a series of parallel walls that are slightly offset to the direction of the roads and the other lots. This offsetting and the succession of walls, in which only indispensable openings have been made, represent a design choice that is strongly indicative of the house's exceptional form and position in relation to the context.

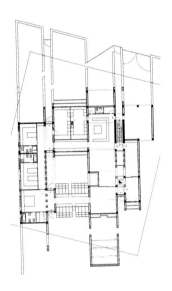

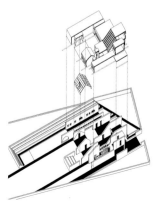

Interior of the villa, with parallel brick walls, the ground floor plan and axonometry of the architectural layout.

Musée d'Orsay, Paris, 1980-1986

with Valerie Bergeron, Monique Bonadei, Giuseppe Raboni, Luc Richard, Marc Vareille and with Emanuela Brignone (1982), Marco Buffoni (1982), Colette Chehab (1981-1982), François Cohen (1984), Nasrine Faghih (1981), André Friedli (1982-1984), Pietro Ghezzi (1980-1982), François Lemaire (1984-1985), Yves Murith (1983), Margherita Palli (1983), Italo Rota (1981-1985), Jean-Marc Rufieux (1981-1983), Gérard Saint Jean (1984), Takashi Shimura (1980-1982), Federico Zürcher (1982)
Lighting Design: Piero Castiglioni

From a theoretical point of view, the fundamental principles of the project can be summarized as follows:

1. When tackling the work, no reference was ever made to methodologies concerning different methods of reuse, but instead attention was focused on an analytical and articulated observation of the two existing "bodies" on which the project was based: the form and typology of Laloux's station building and the museological program for the collections and their layout drawn up by Michel Laclotte.

2. The museological program, the detailed analysis of the works, their groupings and

logical rhythms resulted in a set of rules that meant that the reconstruction of the museum itinerary as a whole was the sum of the typologies specific to the tradition of the various museums: rooms, galleries, and passageways, transfigured by the different formulations imposed by their setting in Laloux's building. This in turn imposed rules on the program, leading to the recognition of different typological units, but at the same time allowing the invention of other types of spaces, like the "Towers," buildings within the building.

3. Laloux's building, its stone walls that alternatively disclose or disguise the iron

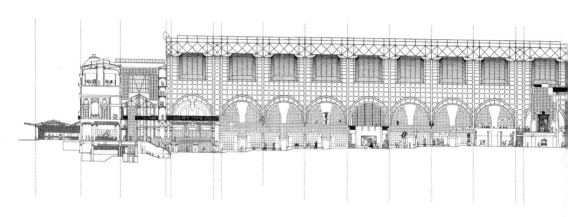

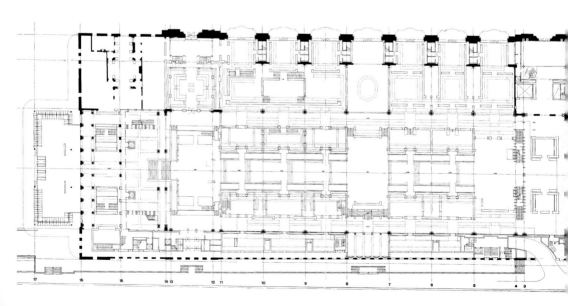

frame, the plasterwork, and the decorations set the "territory for the new construction." The existing building was analyzed as a contemporary object, one without a history; this explains why the principle underlying the composition acted through systematic opposition rather than through stylistic continuity.

4. The awareness that the study of lighting and the control of natural light define the architecture of a museum led to an analysis of the various spaces that the museological itinerary would create, isolating them and articulating the different possibilities for lighting engineering, defined by the common denominator of "indirect light."

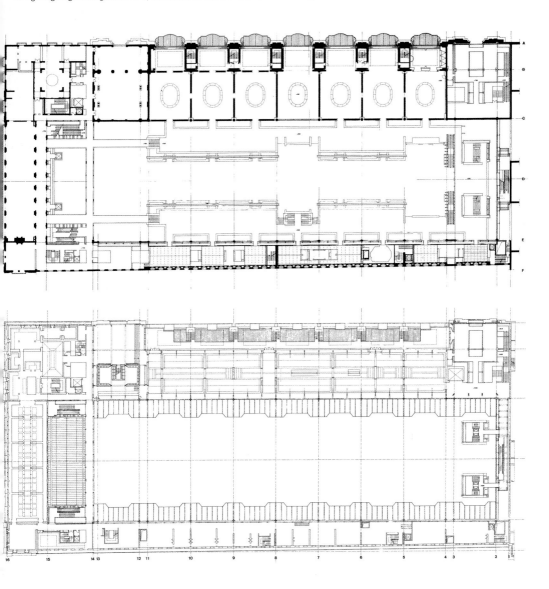

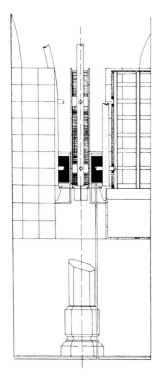

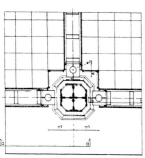

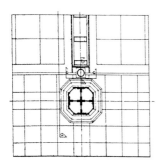

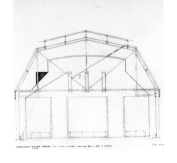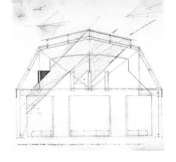

National Museum of Modern Art, Georges Pompidou Centre, Paris, 1982-1985

with Monique Bonadei, Marco Buffoni, Italo Rota, Takashi Shimura, Chiara Vitali
Lighting Design: Piero Castiglioni

The Pompidou Center was regarded as a terrain with its own form, in which the structural rules released the force that generated the new exhibition system. From a museological and an architectural point of view, the interaction between them gave rise to adjustments and subsequent verification. In the new museum the works of art are arranged in closed and formally defined rooms, spaces that are specifically conceived for the enjoyment and understanding of the works. The linguistic neutrality that accompanies the project tends to conceal the visual dimensions of the architecture; only its spatial quality is affirmed.

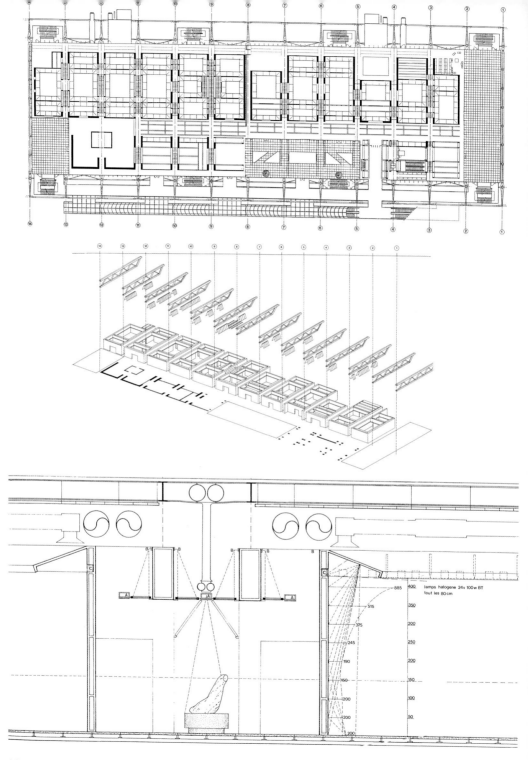

lamps halogene 24v 100w BT
tout les 80 cm

885   400
515   350
375   300
245   250
190   200
150   150
200   100
200   50
200

National Museum of Catalan Art, Barcelona, 1985-2004

with Valerie Bergeron
Monique Bonadei (1985-1996), Marco Della Porta (2000-2001), Anna Escudero
(1990-1992), Angela Gori (1990-1996), Anne Imbert (2000-2001), Fernanda Matas
(2000-2001), Giuseppe Raboni (1985-1993)
and with Enric Steegman and Josep Benedito
Lighting Design: Piero Castiglioni and Installaciones Arquitectoniques (2000-2004)

The project, which started in 1985 and is still in progress, involves the Palau Nacional, built as the ceremonial venue for the 1929 Universal Exposition. The museum will house Catalan works of art from the Romanesque period up to the avant-garde movements of the twentieth century. Only one part of the museum has been built to date and it contains the apses and murals from Romanesque churches in the Pyrenees, as well as works from the Gothic period also on the ground floor. The palace includes a large reception room, a dome, and bell towers, all decorated in a very academic style, but with spaces that promise a strong definition of

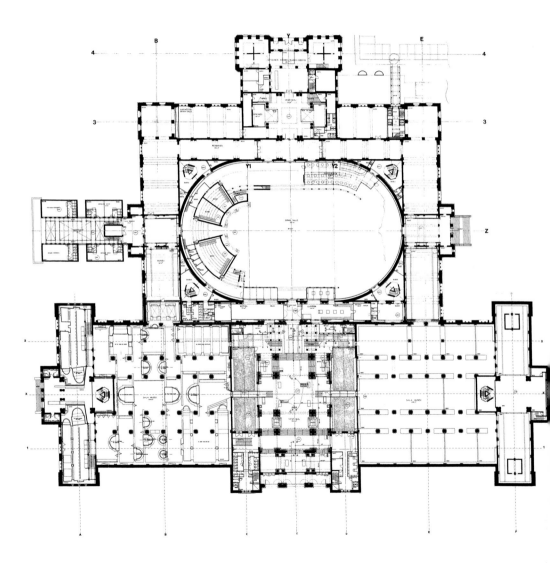

the future museum. The large central hall will be like a large city square with tiered seats for spectators, a cafeteria, a bookshop, a room for introducing visitors to the museum, and two auditoriums. The entrance lobby, which was previously dark, now contains two patios and, for reasons linked to the structural autonomy of the large hall and the dome, the stairways leading to the first floor were completely re-designed. As a result, light now floods into the entrance hall, which has now acquired dynamic potential. The fact that it opens directly onto the external podium, under which lies the technical systems control room, means that a panoramic

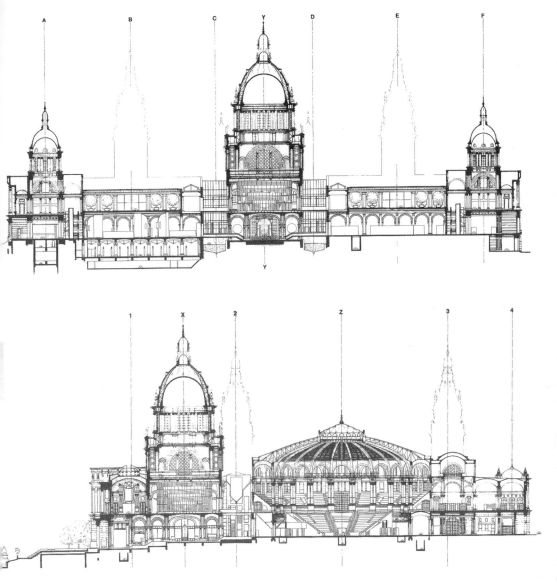

view of the city of Barcelona can be seen from inside the museum. The major re-building works, external constructions, and the large hall were completed in 1992, followed by the museum rooms dedicated to Romanesque art in 1995. The muse-um is now expected to be completed by 2004, including the storages, offices, restoration workshops, a documentation centre, the library, and exhibition spaces.

"Città degli Studi" and detached campus of Turin Polytechnic, Biella, 1987-2000

with Piero Russi, Marco Buffon
Lighting Design: Piero Castiglioni

The program encompasses the construction of a series of buildings, linked to training and research in the textile sector, in the area straddling the main road from Biella to Ivrea, and on the same site, the construction of a detached campus for the textile Engineering Faculty of Turin Polytechnic.

House in Saint-Tropez, 1990

with Valerie Bergeron, Marco Buffoni, Chiara Vitali and Philippe Castanier

The project was conditioned by strong constraints imposed by building regulations (sloped and tiled roof, minimum cubature, a preference for the Provençal style) and the idea of a house in separate parts, based on four elementary cubes linked both internally and externally. The outdoor spaces are designed as part of the house. Overlooking them, the bedrooms open out in a tightly packed sequence of doors and windows framed by square fittings in intense pale blue. The main block of the house forms the corner of a private square, creating a private open-air living room. In the center stands an enormous rock sculpture, while a shady portico on one side closes the basic square.

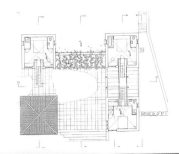

Entrance to Santa Maria Novella Station, Florence, 1990

with Massimo Canevazzi
and with Bianca Ballestrero, Carlo Vannicola
Lighting Design: Piero Castiglioni

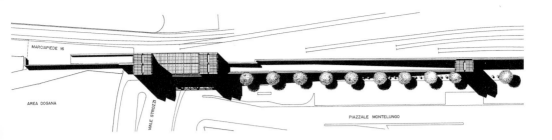

MARCIAPIEDE 16

AREA DOGANA

VIALE STROZZI

PIAZZALE MONTELUNGO

The creation of the new entrance to Santa Maria Novella Station from the piazza beside the Fortezza da Basso followed the recent construction of a vast above-ground car park. It is now one of the main entrances to the station.

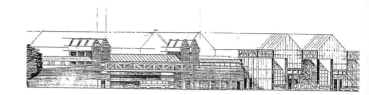

Italian Pavilion at EXPO '92, Seville, 1992

with Vittoria Massa, Marco Buffoni, Raffaella Pirini
and with Pierluigi Spadolini
Lighting Design: Piero Castiglioni

The Universal Expositions, with their pavilions exalting the promotion of trade and progress, have always represented and flanked the major processes of industrialization and modernization in the history of modern civilization, contributing permanent elements to the development of the city. The design for the Italian pavilion is reminiscent of this great tradition. The building is surrounded by a high wall, like the city walls of many Italian fortified towns and also like the many buildings of Arab architectural design present in Seville. This large rectangular enclosure (90 x 50 m), with its tightly woven regular framework, acts as a filter to the real exhibition area, offer-

ing shade and shelter from the noise and traffic of the city. It opens at the base with an arcade that runs down the two long sides, while a series of openings provides glimpses of the interior; the wall divides to allow visitors to enter on one side and cars on the other. On each of the short sides is a waterfall. There are four small internal skylight shafts at the corners, where it is possible to look up to the sky. Inside the wall, the building itself stands on a sheet of water. The entrances are symbolically marked by the four towers that, together with the top gallery, are the only protruding features, marking the building's presence from a distance.

New Asian Art Museum
of San Francisco, 1996-2003

with Vittoria Massa, Milena Archetti, Valerie Bergeron, Marco Buffoni,
Massimiliano Caruso, Francesca Fenaroli
In association with the joint venture Hellmuth, Obata & Kassabaum (HOK) / LDA
Architects / Robert Wong Architect, San Francisco

The Asian Art Museum of San Francisco is one of the largest Western collections of Asian art, established in 1966 following the donation of the Brundage collection, that numbers over 12,000 works. Owned by the City and County of San Francisco, the Museum is jointly managed by the Asian Art Commission and the Asian Art Museum Foundation. With the help of private and public contributions, the museum has successfully been transferred from Golden Gate Park to the Civic Center. The project to transform the Beaux-Arts building of the Old Main Library (1917) now provides 15,000 sqm. for exhibitions and museum activities, focused on unique works of Asian art.

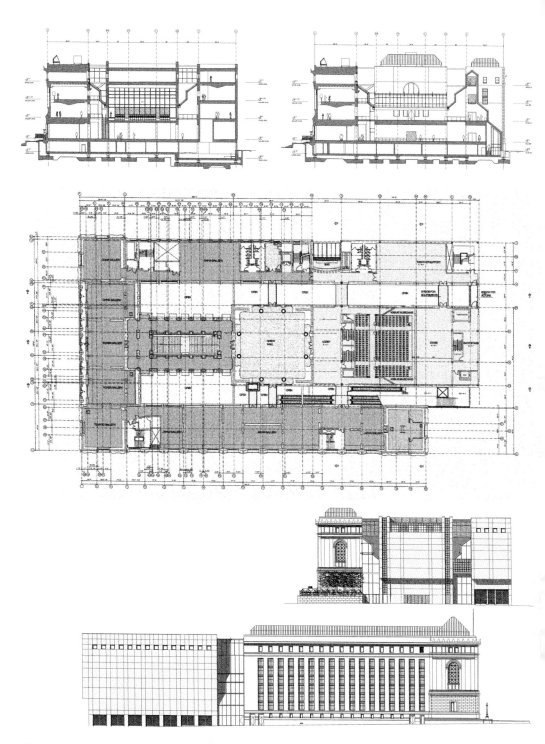

Extension for a Hotel in Jerusalem, 1998-in progress

with Vittoria Massa
and with Arnold Tadjer, Gideon Yeger

The redesign of the existing hotel (built inside the historic English hospital building) and its extension has been accomplished using a series of blocks that repeat the dimensions of the existing layout and are distributed to form an amphitheater that follows the morphology of the land.

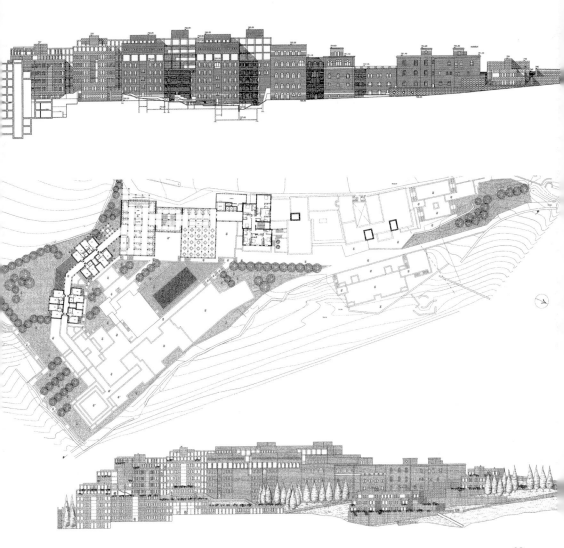

Edoardo Chiossone Civic Museum of Oriental Art, Genoa, 1999-in progress

with Carlo Lamperti, Archicat Srl
Lighting Design: Piero Castiglioni

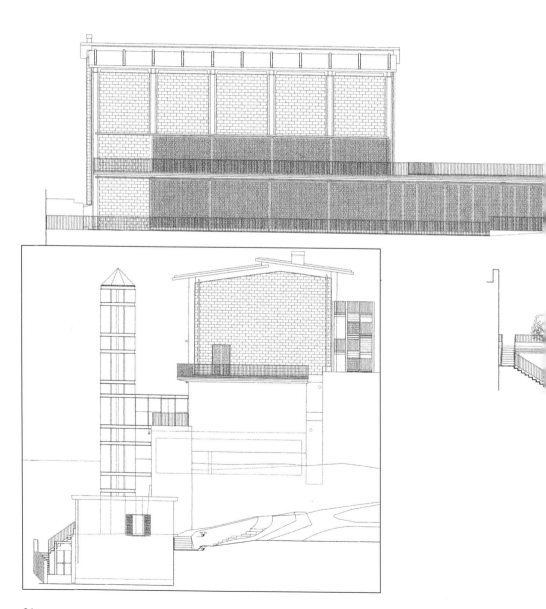

Following a competition, the task of making functional changes and redefining the exhibition layout for the Chiossone Museum was awarded by Genoa City Council. The project was guided by two key figures: the architect Mario Labò, who designed the museum, built in 1971, with a rationalist-type architectural structure whose dynamics had to be integrated in the new project; and Edoardo Chiossone. A painter and engraver from Genoa, Chiossone lived for many years in Japan during the late nineteenth century where he developed a profound interest in Oriental art. He subsequently gifted his entire collection of over 15,000 works to his native city.

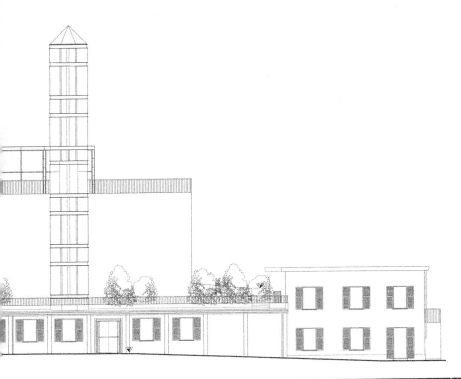

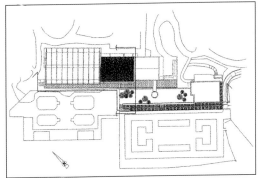

"Museo" and "Dante" stations on Underground Line 1 and redesign of Piazza Cavour and Piazza Dante, Naples, 1999-2002

with Vittoria Massa, Marco Buffoni, Chiara Costa
and with Metropolitana di Napoli SpA

Located in the old city center, Piazza Cavour and Piazza Dante differ considerably in terms of their town-planning and architectural features. Piazza Cavour, with its heterogeneous setting comprising buildings of different qualities, required a uniform intervention that would restore the character of a defined and

settled urban space. The piazza has been redesigned to create a whole garden that, without interruption, forms a sort of large roundabout including a number of architectural features: the "Museo" underground station, a bar, the post office, and the new railway station (*photos above*). On the contrary, Piazza Dante forms a homogeneous urban setting of exceptional character: the project is based on respect for Vanvitelli's hemicycle, whose geometry sets the design of the new paving, whereas the architecture is focused "below ground" (*photos below*), only attempting a dialogue with the existing place structure through the two external exit points.

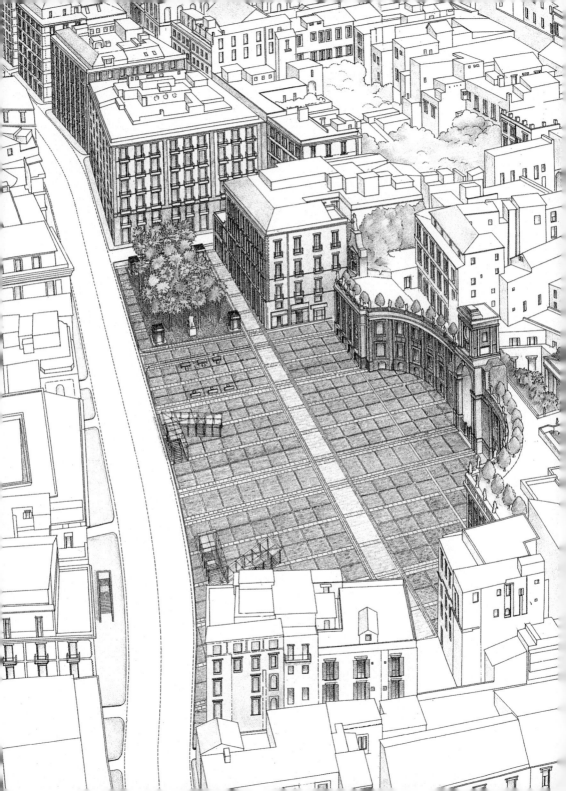

Hotel and tourist development in the province of Taranto, 2000-in progress

with Vittoria Massa, Massimiliano Caruso

The project includes the restoration of an 18th-century farmhouse. The reception services for the hotel, a restaurant, and an archaeological museum are all housed inside the old farmhouse. Small apartments and a botanical garden are planned in the surrounding property, stretching over 78 hectares.

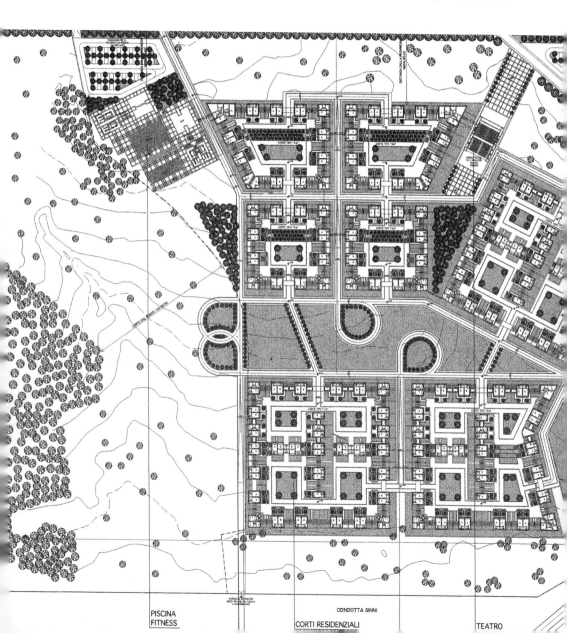

PISCINA
FITNESS

CONDOTTA SINNI

CORTI RESIDENZIALI

TEATRO

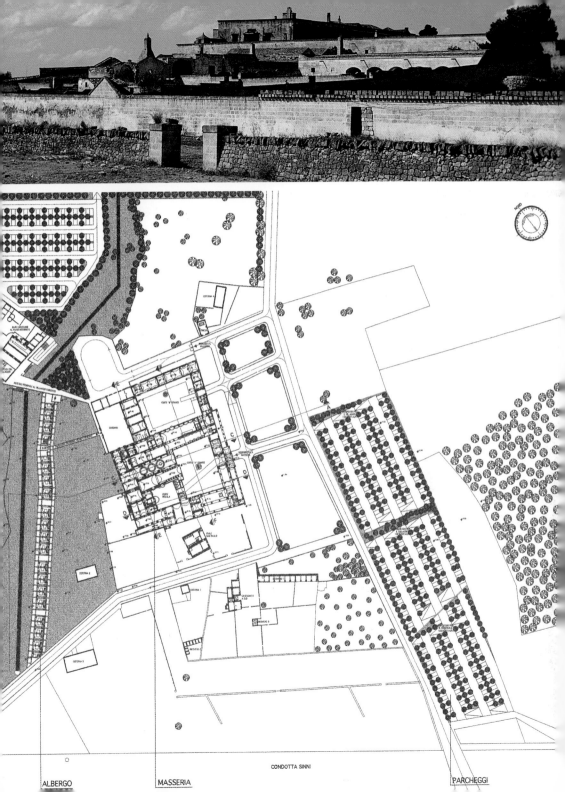

ALBERGO   MASSERIA   CONDOTTA SINNI   PARCHEGGI

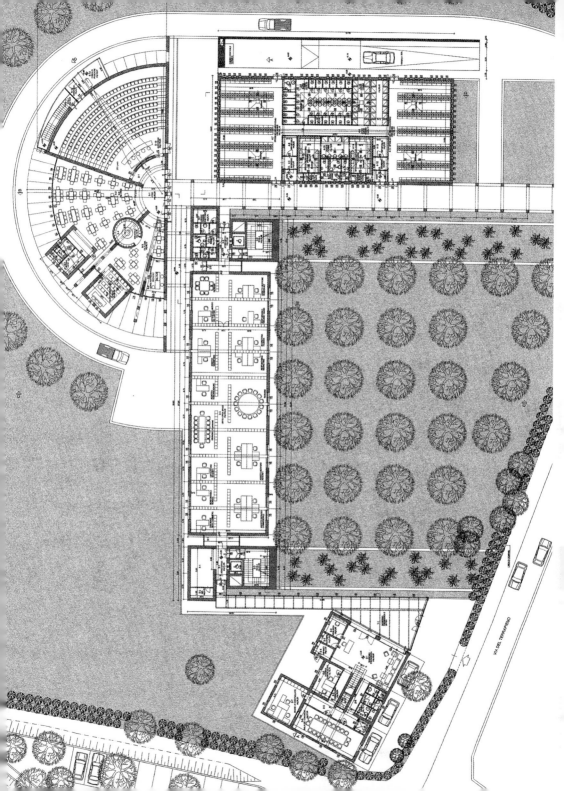

New office headquarters in Rimini, 2001-in progress

with Marco Buffoni

The project regards the construction of an office building, multipurpose leisure and service spaces for the employees, and the renovation of a rural building to house the top management. The new spaces are laid out around a courtyard facing the existing building.

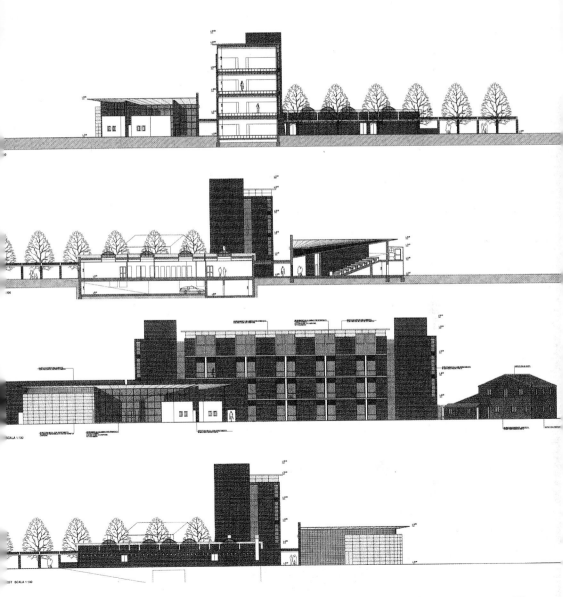

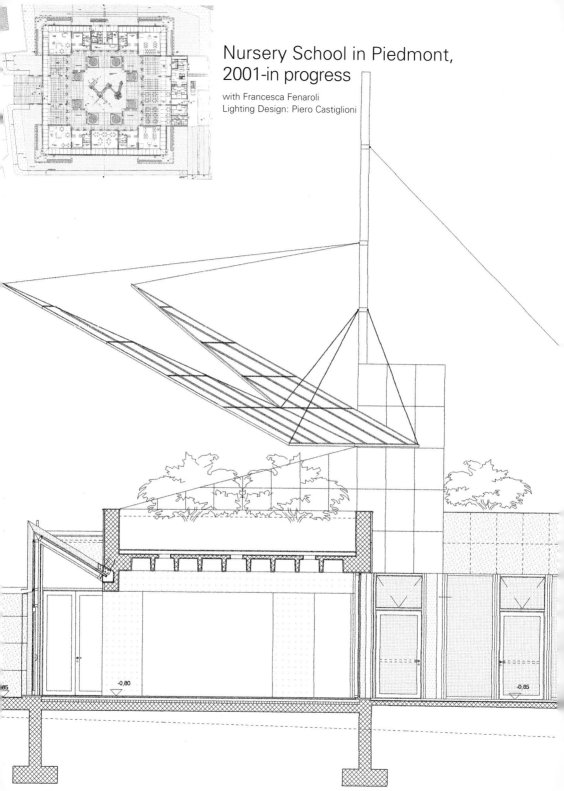

Nursery School in Piedmont, 2001-in progress

with Francesca Fenaroli
Lighting Design: Piero Castiglioni

-0,80

-0,85

The layout of the school is based on new didactic and pedagogical methods. It offers an innovative solution by placing "sails" at the four corners of the building, containing solar panels that will generate clean electricity, making the whole structure virtually autonomous. The square single-storey building has a central courtyard with glazed doors and windows. The four corner classrooms and the various school activities are connected by a corridor running around the perimeter of the building. The atrium leads into the central garden, offering every pupil a chance to play outdoors.

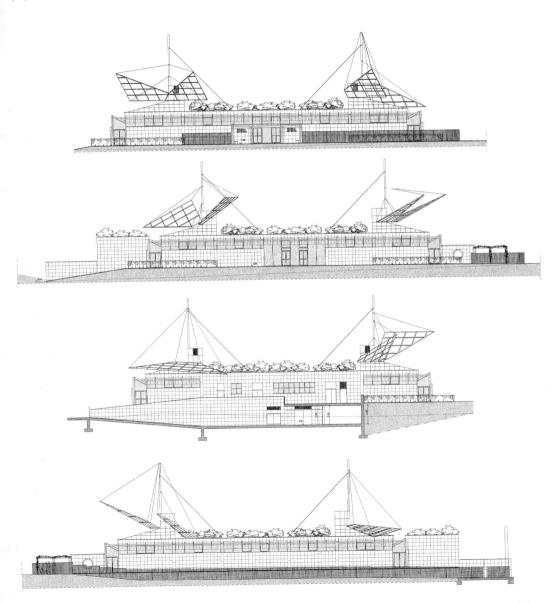

Villa Capriati in Bari, Contemporary Arts and Design Gallery, 2001-in progress

with Vittoria Massa

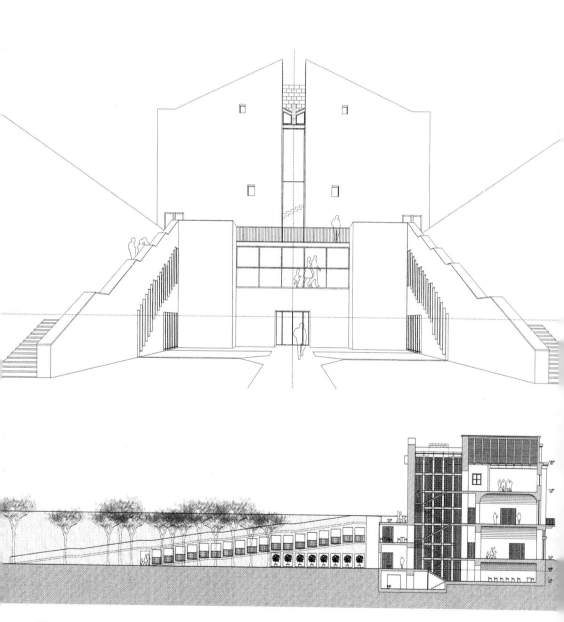

The villa's position beside a road with heavy traffic, its proximity to a recently con-
structed building, and the presence of a pinewood and a large garden at the back
prompted two design approaches: first, to switch the entrance from the front to
the back; and second, to enclose the building between two high plastered walls,
creating a sort of secret garden, a place of silence and meditation before visiting
the gallery. Inside, the spaces are offset at different levels and are accessed from
the new stair, designed as an open space that is visible from the façade and lit
from above, creating a sort of architectural promenade.

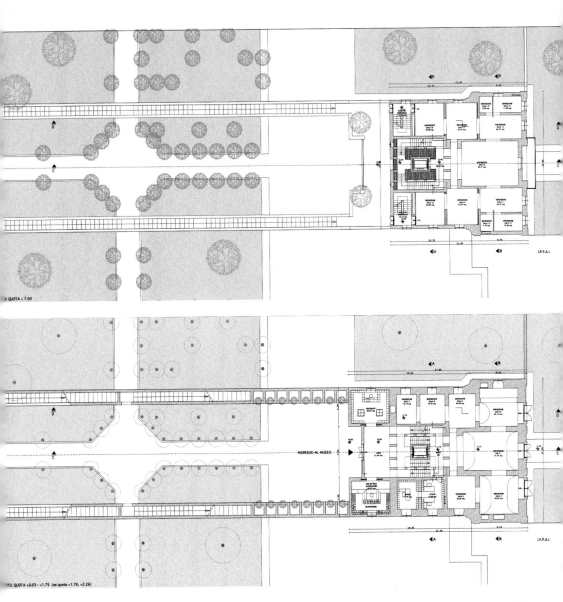

New lakeside promenade in Meina (Novara), 2001-in progress

with Vittoria Massa
and with Gaetano Lisciandra

The promenade runs parallel to the main road, but at a lower level. Two towers with bridges, respectively opposite the European Design Foundation and the parish church, identify the two main architectural features of the town center.

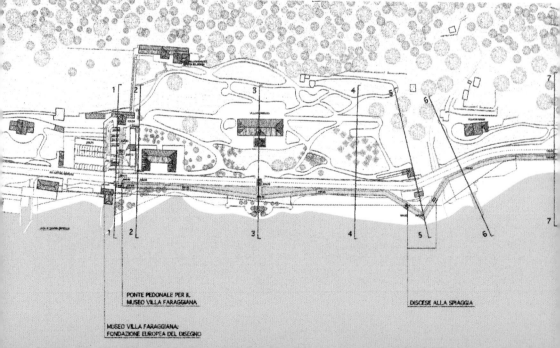

PONTE PEDONALE PER IL
MUSEO VILLA FARAGGIANA

DISCESE ALLA SPIAGGIA

MUSEO VILLA FARAGGIANA:
FONDAZIONE EUROPEA DEL DISEGNO

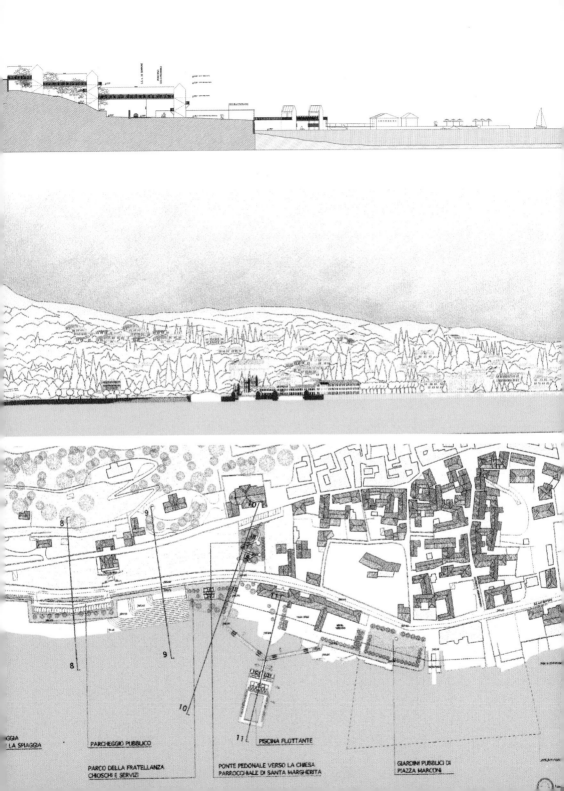

8

9

8

9

10

11

GGIA
LA SPIAGGIA

PARCHEGGIO PUBBLICO

PISCINA FLOTTANTE

PARCO DELLA FRATELLANZA
CHIOSCHI E SERVIZI

PONTE PEDONALE VERSO LA CHIESA
PARROCCHIALE DI SANTA MARGHERITA

GIARDINI PUBBLICI DI
PIAZZA MARCONI

EVOCATIONS

Studies for Aristophanes' *Utopia*, 1974-1975

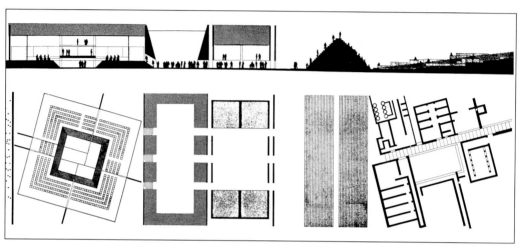

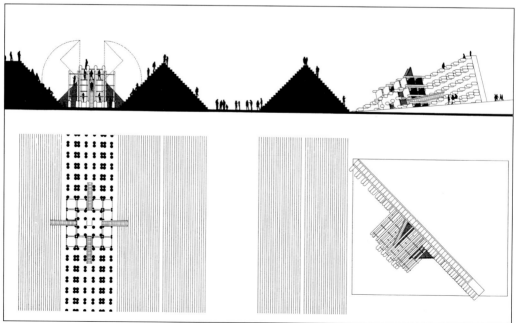

Theater Planning Workshop, Prato, 1976-1978

Director: Luca Ronconi
Studies for *La vita è sogno* by Calderón de la Barca, 1976-1978
The Bacchae by Euripedes, Istituto Magnolfi, Prato, 1978
Calderón by Pier Paolo Pasolini. Teatro Metastasio, Prato, 1978
La Torre by Hugo von Hofmannsthal. Il Fabbricone, Prato, 1978

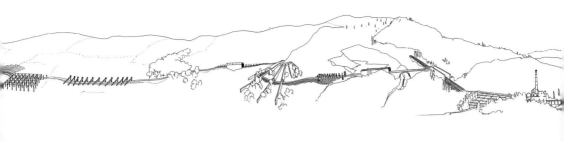

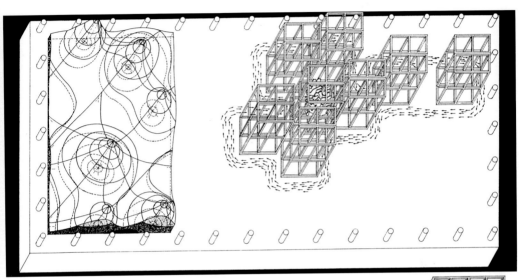

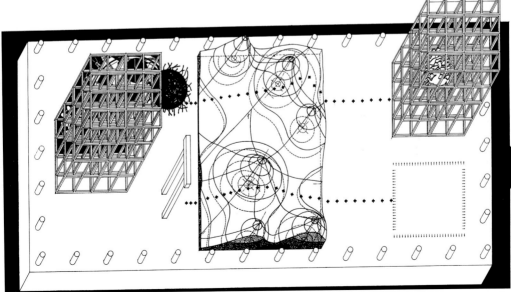

The activities of the Theater Planning Workshop, directed by Luca Ronconi, started in Prato in the summer of 1976 and continued for three years. The following individuals collaborated with the workshop: Gae Aulenti on figurative and territorial research; Franco Quadri on documentation; Dacia Maraini on linguistic research; Ettore Capriolo on the adult literacy course linked to the Workshop. Paolo Radaelli was in charge of organization, together with Giovanni Arnone; Romolo Vestri, of technical organisation; twelve actors from the Tuscolano Cooperative collaborated with the workshop, together with the assistant producer, Ugo Tessitore.

The Workshop program, whose general outline was defined by the relationship between theater and territory, aimed to analyze the nature of theatrical communication through the production of performances and the preparation of materials and instruments useful for the final performance of 1978.

La vita è sogno by Calderón de la Barca, *The Bacchae* by Euripedes, *Calderón* by Pier Paolo Pasolini, and *La Torre* by Hugo von Hofmannsthal were the works chosen to analyzse the nature of theatrical communication. Their public performance was scheduled for late spring 1978, but extensive excerpts from *The Bacchae* and *Calderón* were presented as early as June 1977.

page 84:
Euripedes' *The Bacchae*, Istituto Magnolfi, Prato, 1978
page 85:
Studies for *La vita è sogno* by Calderón de la Barca, 1976-1978
pages 86-87:
Calderón by Pier Paolo Pasolini, Teatro Metastasio, Prato, 1978
pages 88-89:
La Torre by Hugo von Hofmannsthal, Il Fabbricone, Prato, 1978

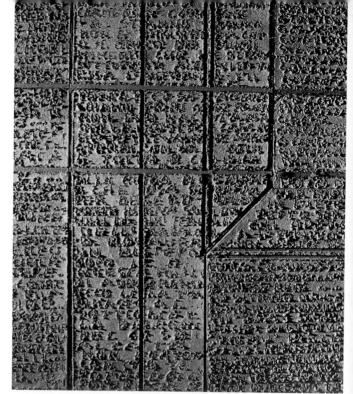

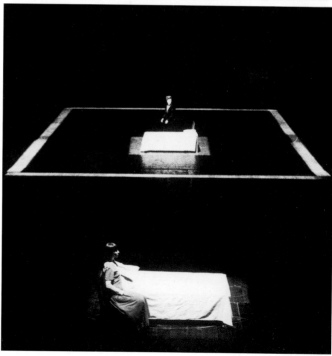

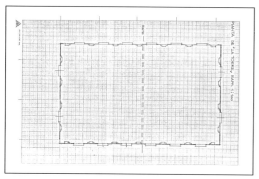

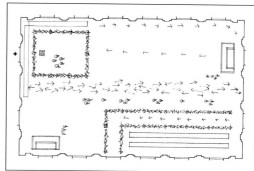

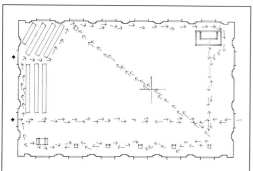

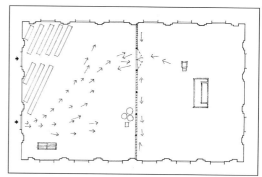

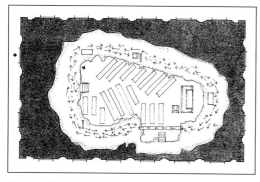

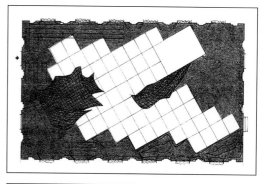

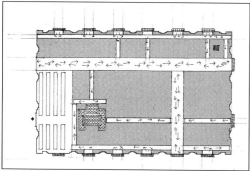

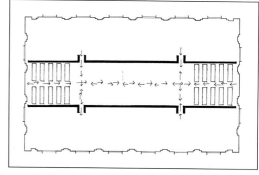

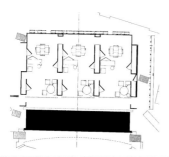

The Wild Duck by Henrik Ibsen, 1977-1978

Director: Luca Ronconi. Costumes: Vera Marzot
1977 Teatro Metastasio, Prato; Teatro Verdi, Pisa; Teatro Duse, Genoa; Teatro Lirico, Milan; Teatro del Palazzo dei Congressi, Bologna; Teatro Comunale, Modena; Teatro Donizetti, Bergamo; Teatro Argentina, Rome
1978 Teatro Alfieri, Turin; Teatro Comunale, Ferrara; Teatro Aligheri, Ravenna

Opera by Luciano Berio, 1979-1980

Conductor: Marcello Panni. Director: Luca Ronconi
Costumes: Giovanna Buzzi
1979 Théâtre de l'Opéra, Lyons; Maison de la Culture, Nanterre (Paris)
1980 Teatro Regio, Turin; Teatro dell'Opera, Rome

Samstag aus Licht and *Donnerstag aus Licht* by Karlheinz Stockhausen, 1984 and 1981

Samstag aus Licht: Conductor: Karlheinz Stockhausen. Director: Luca Ronconi. Costumes: Giovanna Buzzi. Palazzo dello Sport, Milan. Production by Teatro alla Scala, Milan
Donnerstag aus Licht: Conductor: Peter Eotvos. Director: Luca Ronconi Costumes: Giovanna Buzzi. Teatro alla Scala, Milan

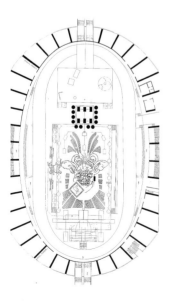

La donna del lago by Gioachino Rossini, 1981-1989

Conductor: Maurizio Pollini. Director and stage designer: Gae Aulenti. Costumes: Giovanna Buzzi
1981 Rossini Opera Festival, Pesaro; 1983 Rossini Opera Festival, Pesaro; 1986 Teatro Comunale Giuseppe Verdi, Trieste; Théâtre de l'Opéra, Nice; 1989 Teatro Regio, Parma

Il viaggio a Reims by Gioachino Rossini, 1984-2001

Conductor: Claudio Abbado. Director: Luca Ronconi. Costumes: Giovanna Buzzi
1984 Auditorium Pedrotti, Rossini Opera Festival, Pesaro; 1985 Teatro alla Scala,
Milan; 1988 Staatsoper, Vienna; 1992 Teatro Comunale, Ferrara; Teatro Rossini,
Rossini Opera Festival, Pesaro
Conductor: Daniele Gatti. 1999 Palafestival, Rossini Opera Festival, Pesaro; 2001
Teatro Comunale, Bologna

Zar Saltan by Nikolaj Rimskij-Korsakov, 1988

Conductor: Vladimir Fedossev. Director: Luca Ronconi. Costumes: Giovanna Buzzi
Teatro Municipale Romolo Valli, Reggio Emilia; Teatro Lirico, Milan
Production by Teatro alla Scala, Milan

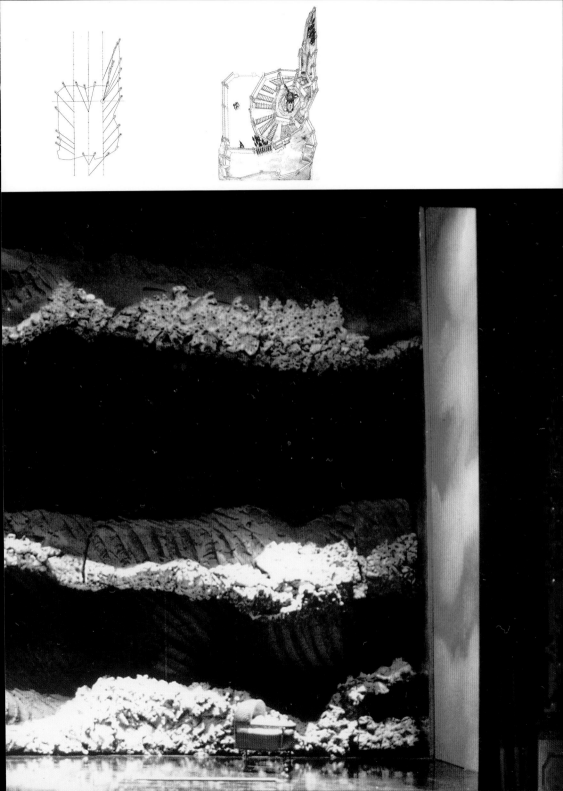

Set for the television programme
Una Storia, 1992
on RAI 1, presented by Enzo Biagi

with Francesca Fenaroli

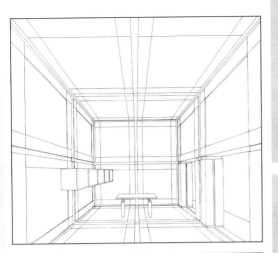

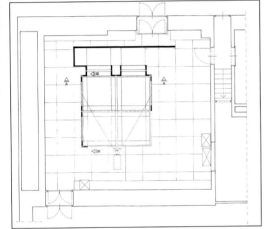

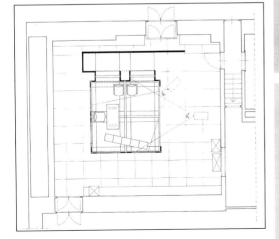

di
ENZO BIAGI

scenografia
GAE AULENTI

Il mondo della Luna
by Franz Joseph Haydn, 1994

Conductor: Salvatore Accardo. Director: Costa Gavras. Costumes: Giovanna Buzzi
Teatro San Carlo, Naples.

Elektra by Richard Strauss, 1994

Conductor: Giuseppe Sinopoli. Director: Luca Ronconi. Costumes: Giovanna Buzzi
Teatro alla Scala, Milan.

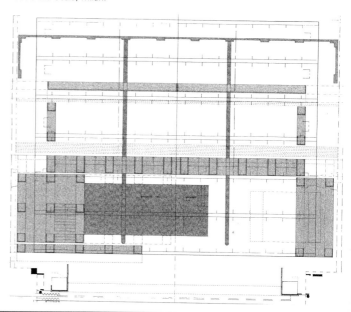

Business School, Oxford, 1996

International invited competition
with Vittoria Massa, Marco Buffoni, Milena Archetti
and with Ove Arup & Partners International, London

St Catherine's

St Cross Church

Zoology and Psychology

Manchester

New College

Wadham

All Souls

Radcliffe Camera

(New) Bodleian Library

Clarendon Bd.

Bodleian Library

Radcliffe Square

St Mary's

Sheldonian Theatre

Brasenose

Blackwells

Trinity

Exeter

Lincoln

Balliol

Broad Street

Jesus

Covered Market

Oxford Story

St Michael's Church

Carfax Tower

High Street

The invited competition announced by Oxford University was for a new international Business School in the city center. The project included a four-sided building facing onto a courtyard divided by a glazed passageway, providing a transparent transversal axis, a fundamental space for distribution and orientation, running from the main entrance to the sports ground. The four corner towers, with glazed roofs for natural ventilation, provide the vertical link between the various functions distributed throughout the four floors of the building. The terrace along the east wing offers additional space for the social life of the faculty.

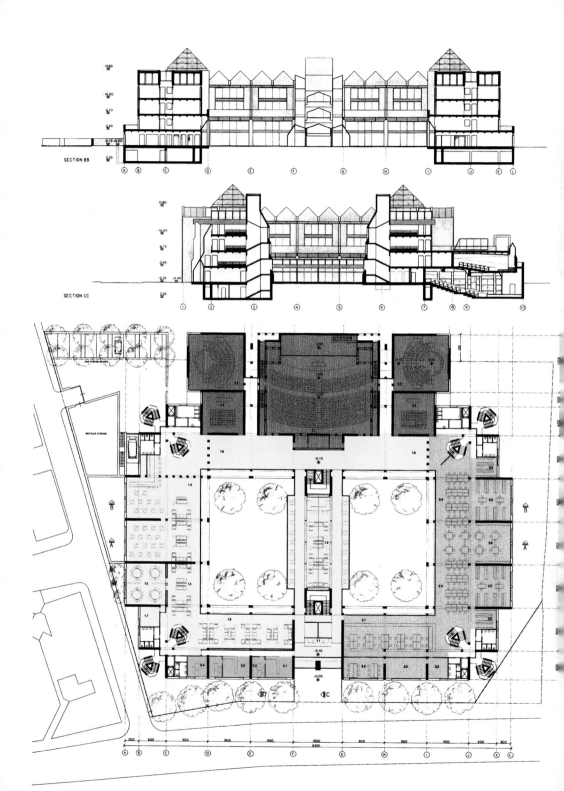

SECTION BB

SECTION CC

THE COURTYARD

VIEW FROM SPORTS GROUND TOWARD TERRACE

DETAIL OF NORTHWEST CORNER OF BUILDING

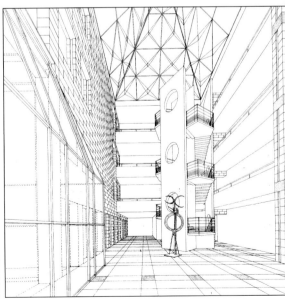

PERSPECTIVE VIEW OF INTERIOR

Piazza Ciullo and Piazza del Mercato at Alcamo (Trapani), 1996-in progress

with Marco Buffoni
Lighting Design: Piero Castiglioni

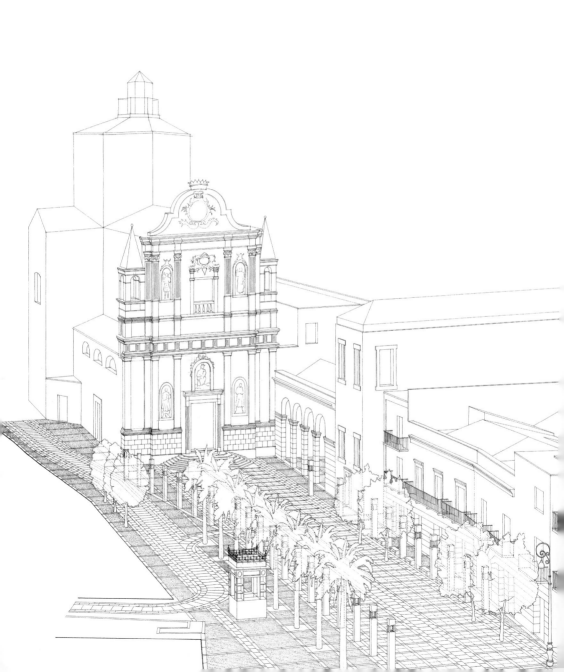

By designing new paving and new simple street furnishings, the project aims to interrelate the existing public buildings and to emphasise the pattern and intersection of the various urban structures that converge on the square.

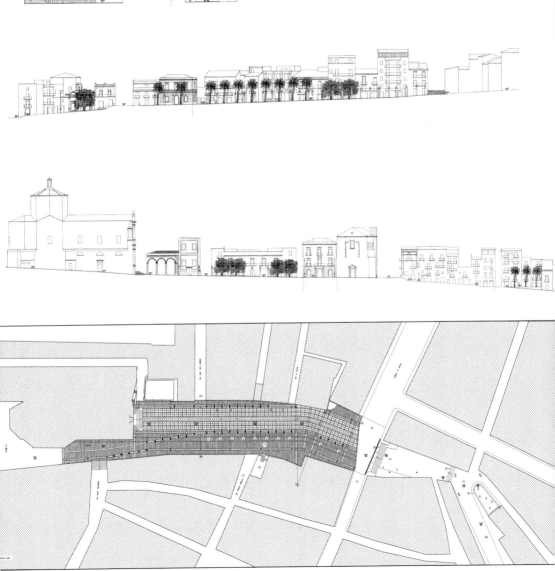

Renovation of National Gallery of Victoria, Melbourne, 1996

International competition
with Vittoria Massa, Marco Buffoni
and with Denton Corker Marshall Pty Ltd., Melbourne

The project provides a series of new elements in basic geometric forms, to be built using materials and colors that differ from the dark stone of the existing building, highlighting their add-on quality and offering the opportunity to create a strong new image for the Gallery.

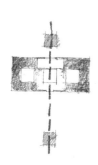

PERMANENT   CIRCULATION   TEMPORARY

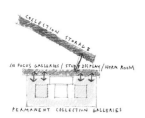

COLLECTION STORAGE

IN FOCUS GALLERIES / STUDY DISPLAY / WORK ROOM

PERMANENT COLLECTION GALLERIES

EDUCATION   VISITOR SERVICES

← DEVELOPMENT (AT UPPER LEVEL)

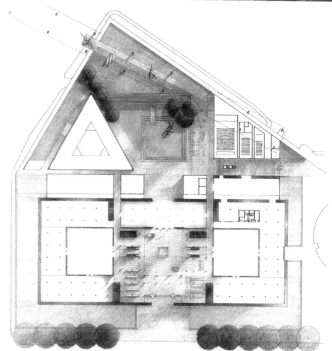

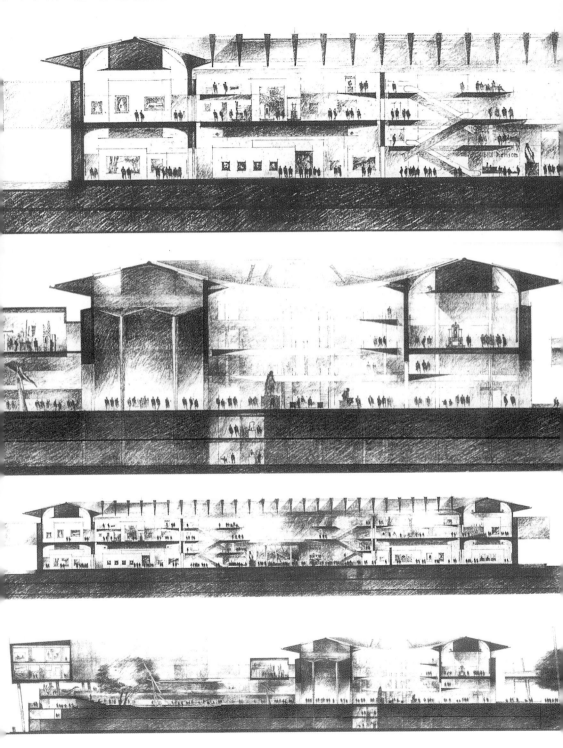

La Fenice Theatre, Venice, 1997

International tender-competition for reconstruction
with Marco Buffoni, Francesca Fenaroli, Vittoria Massa, Milena Archetti

Temporary Grouping of Companies: Impregilo SpA, Fiatengineering, ICCEM Srl, CO.VE.CO, SACAIM SpA

ARCHITECTURAL PROJECT

Gae Aulenti, Margherita Petranzan (also responsible for the historical-critical study), Antonio Foscari

Computer drawings: Carlo Lamperti - Archicat Srl (Milan)

Representation of decorative and geometric components: Sandi Torsello Associati (Venice)

Analysis of materials and textures: Francesco Amendolagine and Giuseppe Boccanegra, Consorzio Artigiano "La Nuova Fenice" (Venice)

Style decorations and furnishings: Renzo Mongiardino (Milan)

Color research: Eliana Gerotto (Venice)

Lighting engineering: Piero Castiglioni (Milan)

STRUCTURAL ENGINEERING

Renato Vitaliani (Padua)

Chemical-physical consolidation: Enzo Ferroni (Florence)

Masonry consolidation: Giorgio Macchi (Florence)

Geotechnical Engineering: Alberto Mazzuccato (Padua)

Structural calculation: Filippo Navarra (Padua); Giorgio Serafini (Venice)

ELECTROMECHANICAL SYSTEMS

Fiatengineering (Turin)

ACOUSTIC DESIGN

Müller B.B.M., Munich

THEATRICAL MACHINERY DESIGN

Fiat engineering (Turin)

Stage machinery and Theatrical technologies: Silvano Cova (Turin)

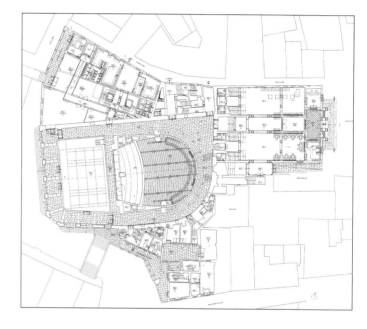

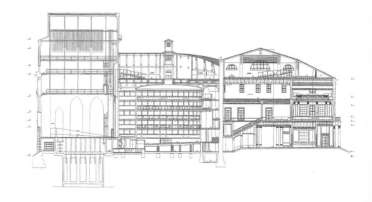

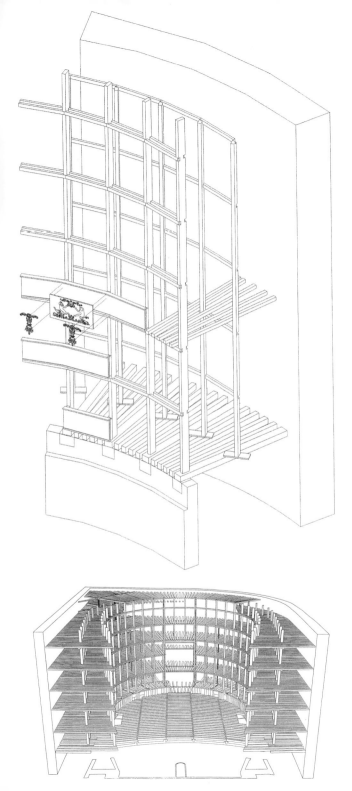

1792 Inauguration of theater. Project by Giannantonio Selva.

1836 Large part of theater destroyed by fire.

1837 New inauguration of theater. Project by Tommaso and Giambattista Meduna.

1859 Theater closed as part of demonstration against Austrian government.

1866 Theater re-opened under Vittorio Emanuele II.

1915 Theater closed after outbreak of First World War.

1938 Inauguration of season following refurbishment by Eugenio Miozzi.

29 January 1996 The theater was again destroyed by fire.

6 February 1996 The Prefect of Venice, Giovanni Troiani, was appointed "Commissioner for the reconstruction of the Theater" in order to cope with the disaster.

2 September 1996 The Prefecture of Venice announced the international tender-competition for the reconstruction of the theater. The terms of the call for awarding the contract are:
– Cost of works (basic tender for overall value of rebuilding works, Lire 120 billion)
– Technical and aesthetic value of work
– Running and maintenance costs
– Completion times (within 883 days from date of site opening).

31 March 1997 Projects from the six groups accepted to take part in the bid for tenders were delivered to the Prefecture of Venice:
1. Carena SpA, Genoa with project by Arch. Gino Valle.

2. Consorzio Cooperative Costruzioni, Bologna with project by Arch. Carlo Aymonino and Romeo Ballardini.

3. Ferrovial SA, Madrid with project by Arch. Salvator Perez Arroyo.

4. Philipp Holzmann BAG Sud, Munich with project by Arch. Aldo Rossi.

5. Impregilo SpA, Milan with project by Arch. Gae Aulenti.

6. Mabetex Project Engineering SA, Lugano with project by Arch. Ignazio Gardella and Giuseppe Cristinelli.

31 May 1997 In an order issued by the "Official Commissioner," the reconstruction work was awarded to the Impregilo group.

The groups were ranked with the following scores:

1st Impregilo	70.1
2nd Philipp Holzmann	67.5
3rd Carena	62.9
4th Consorzio C.C.	47.9
5th Mabetex	10.7

The Ferrovial group was excluded by the jury.

27 June 1997 The Prefecture of Venice signed the contract with the Impregilo group and procedeed to "site opening". Works were scheduled for completion by 27 September 1999.

21 October 1997 The Regional Court of Veneto turned down the objections lodged during the previous months by the companies Carena and Philipp Holzmann.

13 February 1998 Following an injunction passed by the Council of State, granting the appeal lodged by Philipp Holzmann, the rebuilding work was immediately suspended.

The underlying motive for the appeal was that the winning project did not take account of private property meas-

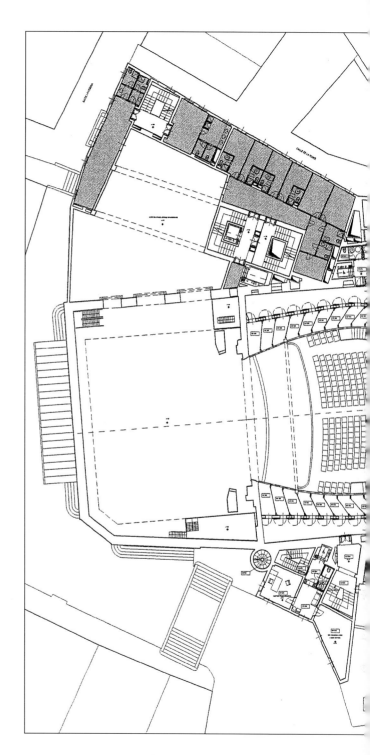

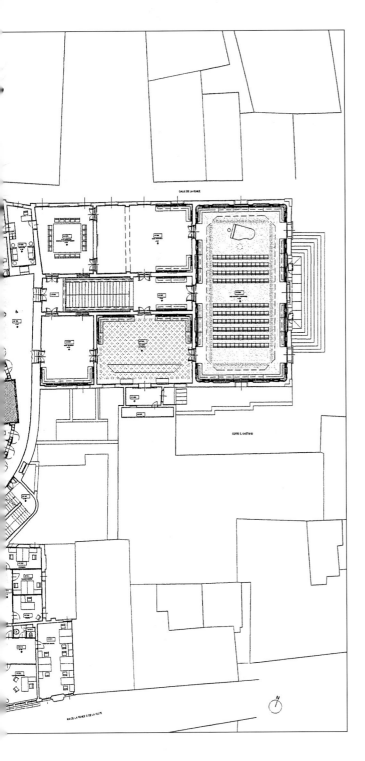

uring some 330 square meters in the southern section of the structural complex.

11 March 1999 In a new order passed by the "Official Commissioner" with the support of the jury, the rebuilding works were awarded to the Philipp Holzmann group.

15 June 1999 A new "assignment of works" was signed with a completion date on 1 October 2001.

21 March 2001 The Mayor of Venice, Paolo Costa, the new "Official Commissioner," terminated the contract with the Holzmann group on the grounds that the company was in breach of contract. The task of adapting the project was then assigned to Aldo Rossi Associati in order to start a new tender procedure.

11 July 2001 A new private bidding process was held to award the executive design for the theatre and the accomplishment of the rebuilding works.

5 October 2001 The contract was awarded to the Temporary Grouping of Companies consisting of Sacaim SpA, Consorzio Cooperative Costruzioni, Gemmo Impianti SpA and Impresa Ing. Mantovani. The works are due to be finished by 30 November 2003.

New Town Hall, San Casciano
in Val di Pesa (Florence), 1997

with Vittoria Massa

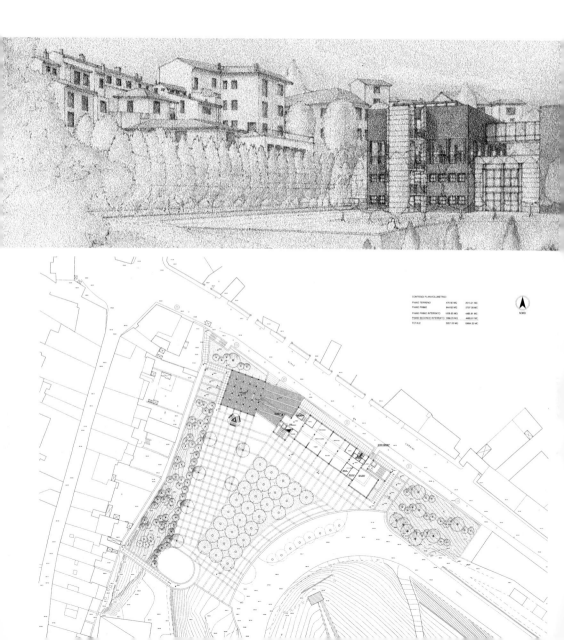

The project site is an area tangent to the historic center, characterized by rapidly sloping ground and overlooking the attractive valley leading into the town. The project aims at redeveloping the area by creating a building with a strong public and urban character, made up of two autonomous sections, in terms of both form and function, divided by an open piazza, which then merge as they extend toward the valley. The bottom area, which is planted with species native to the Tuscan countryside, provides an element of continuity with the landscape.

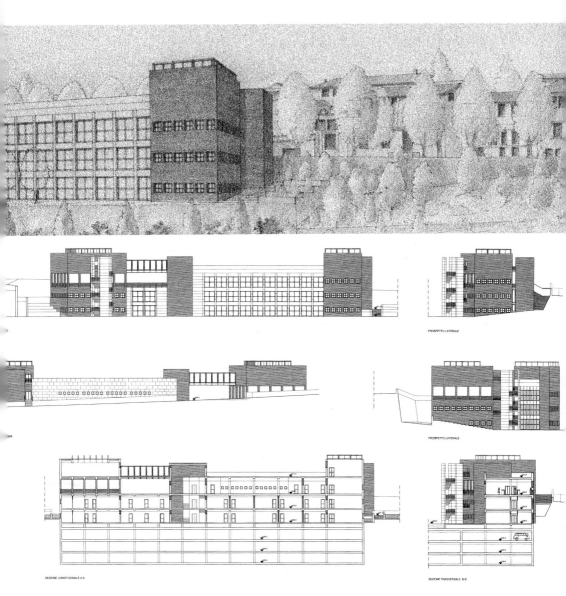

PROSPETTO LATERALE

PROSPETTO LATERALE

SEZIONE LONGITUDINALE A-A

SEZIONE TRASVERSALE B-B

Linhu Villas, Shanghai, 1997

with Marco Buffoni, Vittoria Massa, Chiara Costa
and with Impregilo SpA, Shanghai

The project involves the construction of three villas for a leading hotel in Shanghai. The villas overlook a lake in an area featuring important landscape elements to be definitely preserved.

The buildings are independent, separated by extensive green areas, and feature enclosed courtyards for each residence. At the same time, their connection is organized to ensure that each villa occupies the best position with respect to the site.

New exit from the Uffizi, Piazza Castellani, Florence 1998

International invited consultation
with Vittoria Massa
and with Bianca Ballestrero

VIA DEI CASTELLANI

BIBLIOTEC

N

"Something could be put here to restrain this space that comes forward, like a fountain; then a theme could be created with steps resting on what has already been built." (Giovanni Michelucci)

The project proposes rows of square stone columns standing on a sloping plane which, at a constant inclination, links the exit from the Uffizi Museum with Via Castellani and restores the continuity of the street. This choice takes into account the relatively small dimension of the space, a fact that would have been emphasized if it were fragmented at different levels, altering the relationship with the surrounding buildings.

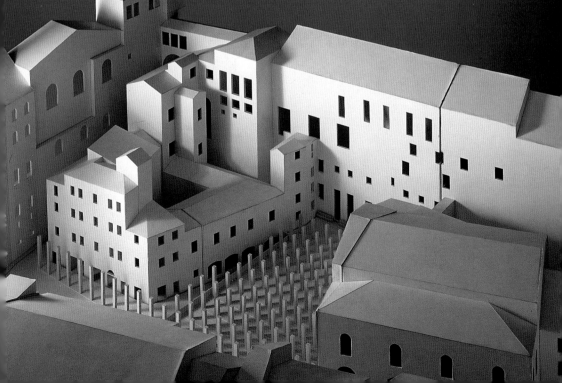

The Museum of Women, The Leadership Center, New York, 2000

International competition
with Marco Buffoni, Vittoria Massa, Milena Archetti
and with Hellmuth, Obata & Kassabaum (HOK), New York

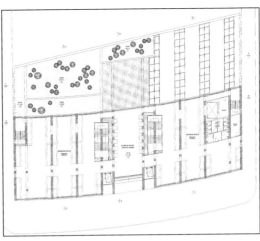

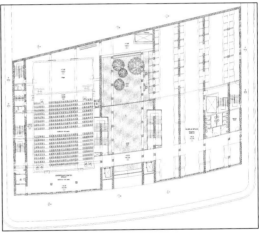

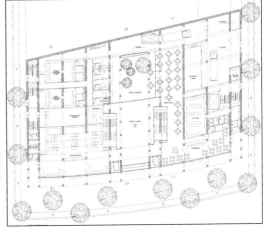

The area of Lower Manhattan assigned for the construction of the new building calls for considerable responsibility in terms of choosing an architecture appropriate to its public and educational function, significant within the predominantly residential complex of Battery Park City, while keeping its relationship with the context.

The museum building follows the curved line of the street, revealing a convex façade along the main front, characterized by a portico which sets the Museum environment and its identity as a public building.

The geometry of the building is based on the intersection of a series of parallel load-bearing walls and circle arcs, forming the structural plot. The use of these two crossed geometrical schemes allows a dynamic perception of the interiors that are defined by the parallel walls but at the same time vary in rhythm and sequence depending on the passages that follow the curved lines. Town-planning requirements impose precise heights and setbacks corresponding to the two distinct functions inside the building: the lower zone is destined for the museum and public activities, the higher floors will be used for offices and curators, and the top floor as the Leadership Center. The centrally placed lobby guarantees a rational distribution of the various functions between the different floors, accessed by two glazed staircases and two lifts.

The project sustains energy efficiency and green-architecture by using natural, non rare, highly efficient materials. Photovoltaic roof panels guarantee that energy requirements are partly met using pollution-free systems.

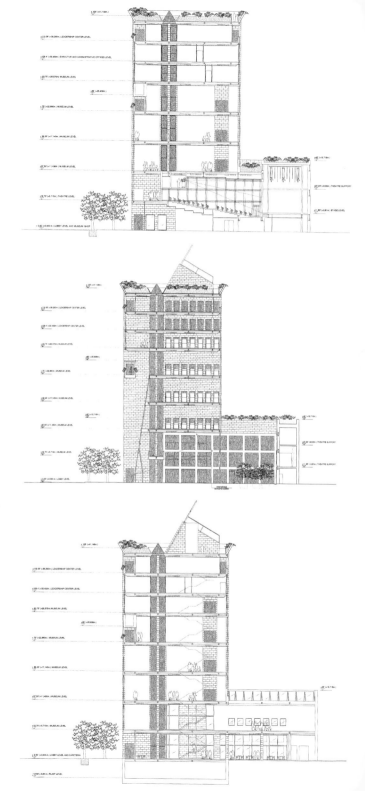

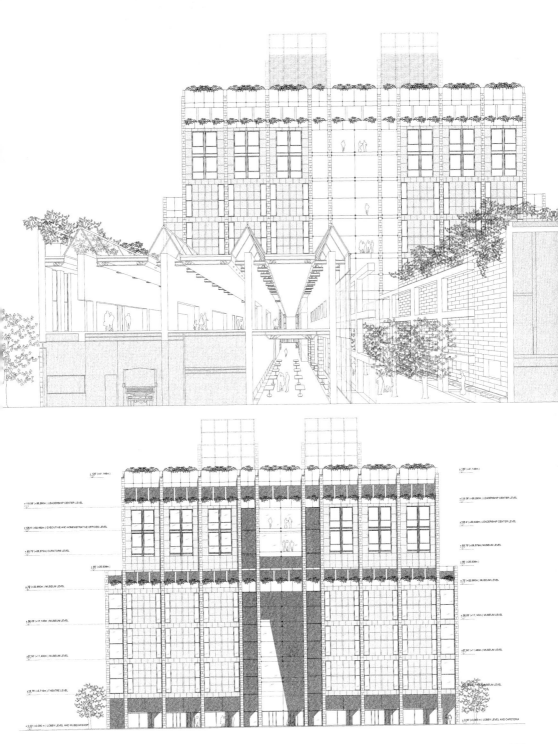

+130' (+41,148m.)

+19,08' (+38,380m.) LEADERSHIP CENTER LEVEL

+106,4' (+32,492m.) EXECUTIVE AND ADMINISTRATIVE OFFICES LEVEL

+93,78' (+28,575m.) CURATORS LEVEL

+85' (+25,908m.)

+,78' (+22,860m.) MUSEUM LEVEL

+56,22' (+17,145m.) MUSEUM LEVEL

+37,50' (+11,430m.) MUSEUM LEVEL

+18,75' (+5,716m.) THEATRE LEVEL

+,00' (±0,000m.) LOBBY LEVEL AND MUSEUM SHOP

+130' (+41,148m.)

+19,08' (+38,380m.) LEADERSHIP CENTER LEVEL

+106,4' (+32,492m.) LEADERSHIP CENTER LEVEL

+93,78' (+28,575m.) MUSEUM LEVEL

+85' (+25,908m.)

+,78' (+22,860m.) MUSEUM LEVEL

+56,22' (+17,145m.) MUSEUM LEVEL

+37,50' (+11,430m.) MUSEUM LEVEL

+,78' (+22,860m.) MUSEUM LEVEL

+5,00' (±0,000m.) LOBBY LEVEL AND CAFETERIA

New factory with offices at Plan-les-Ouates (Geneva), 2001

International invited competition with Marco Buffoni, Vittoria Massa, Chiara Costa and with Serge Vuarraz (Vuarraz Varesio Rosse Architectes), A+Réal Architecture, Michel Paquet (ESM Ingénierie SA), Jacques Kugler and Jean Anderegg (Rigot + Rieben Engineering SA), Albert Ruffert and Gilles Jakubowski (Ingénieur-Conseils Scherler SA), Philippe Bissat (BCS SA)
Lighting Design: Piero Castiglioni

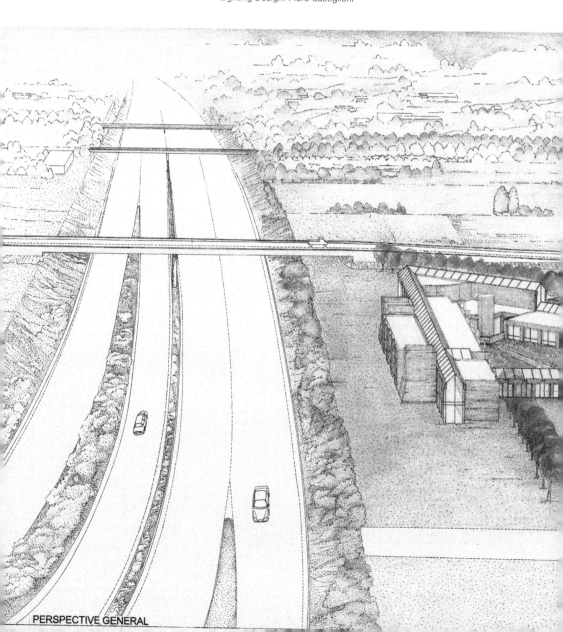

PERSPECTIVE GENERAL

The project area lies very close to the Geneva-Paris motorway, in an extremely visible position surrounded by other industrial buildings. The reputation of this leading company and its artistic and craft products requires that the building is recognizable as a "noble" factory, as well as administrative headquarters. The resulting architecture is simple in its structure, but at the same time articulated and carefully blended into the landscape. It always presents a dynamic perspective that is never the same. The project comprises four units: atrium, factory, offices, and restaurant, as recognizable but integrated and interlinked elements. The two-storey of-

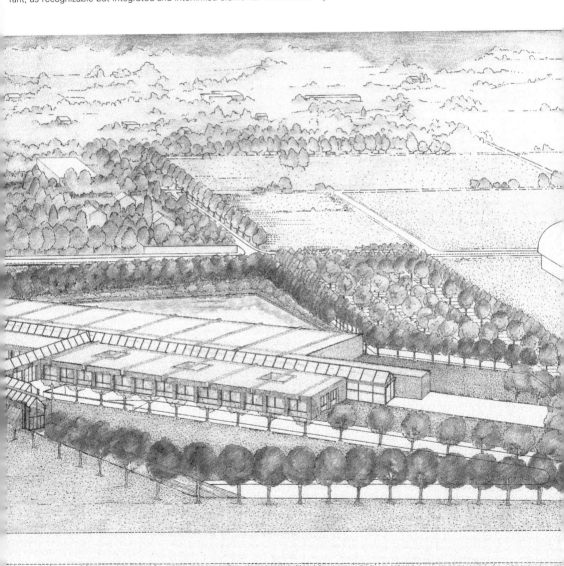

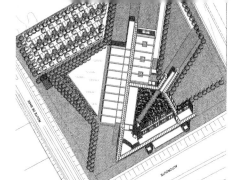

fice complex lies parallel to the motorway. The single-storey factory building rotates in order to capture light from the north. The backbone, which distributes and accompanies all the project elements, consists of a gallery of perforated walls with a glazed roof. All the components of

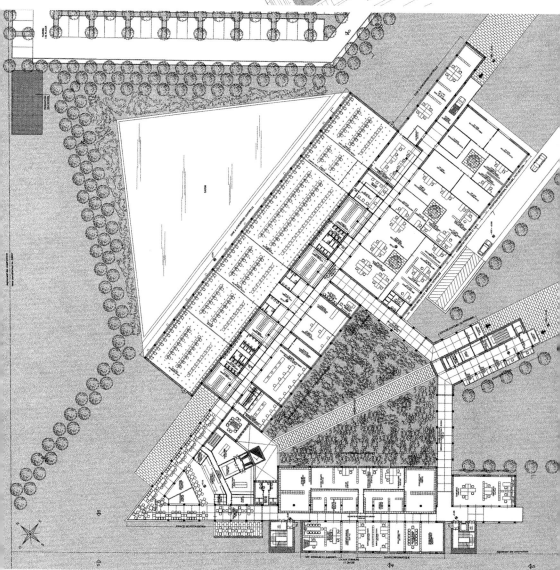

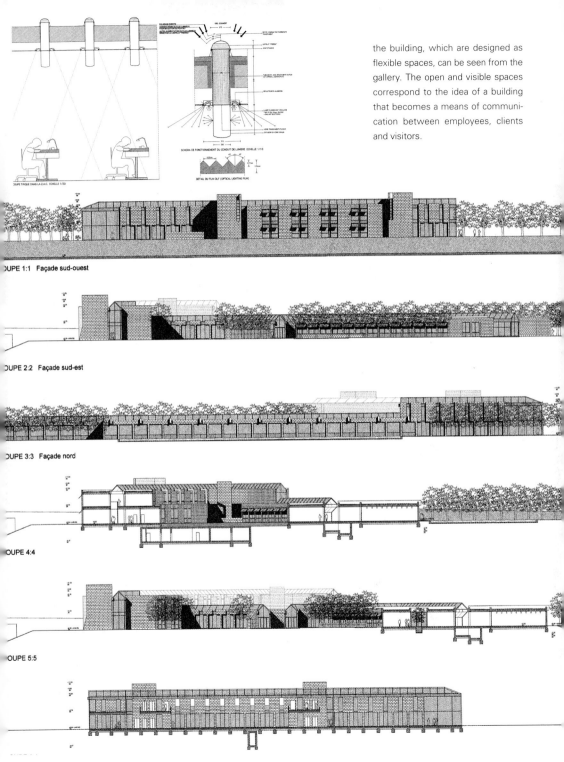

the building, which are designed as flexible spaces, can be seen from the gallery. The open and visible spaces correspond to the idea of a building that becomes a means of communication between employees, clients and visitors.

COUPE 1:1 Façade sud-ouest

COUPE 2:2 Façade sud-est

COUPE 3:3 Façade nord

COUPE 4:4

COUPE 5:5

ORDER
AND
TRANSGRESSION

Holiday Center at the Tonale Pass, 1962

with Tekne SpA

The project involves a large holiday center for use by young persons. It constitutes a complex infrastructure (containing a church, library, post office, basic shops, cinema-theater, and indoor swimming pool) with the aim of revitalizing the entire area.

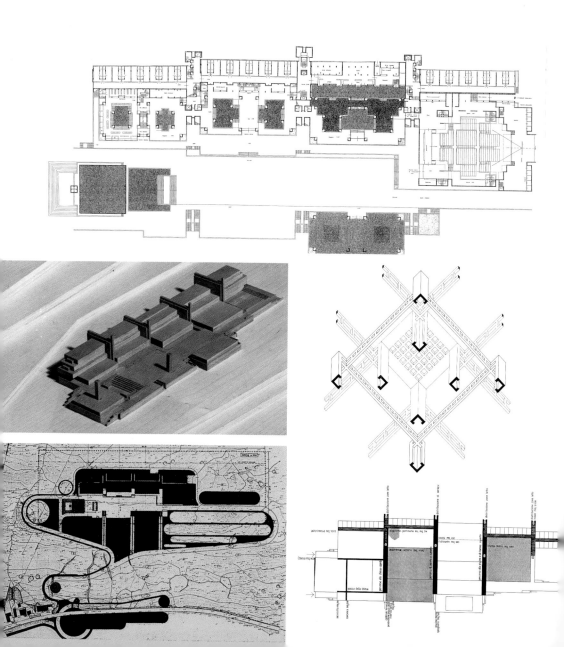

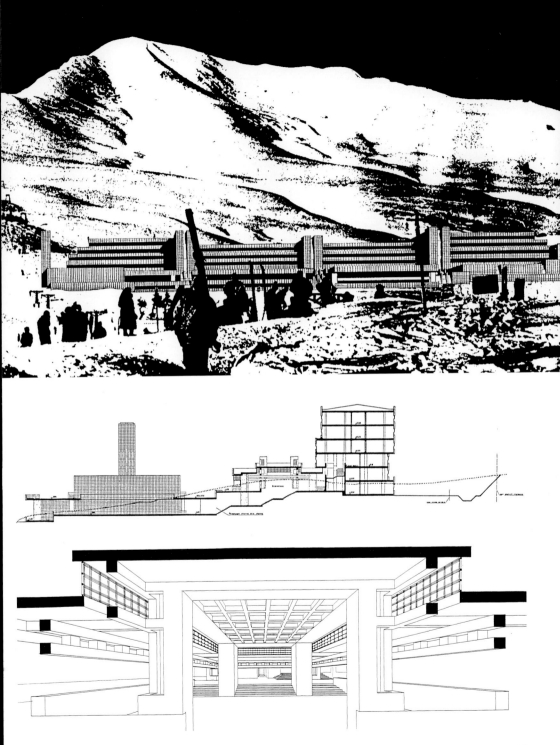

13ᵗʰ Milan Triennale Exhibition, Italian Section, *Il Tempo delle Vacanze*, 1964

International Grand Prix for installation

with Carlo Aymonino, Stefano Paciello and Ezio Bonfanti, Jacopo Gardella, Cesare Macchi Cassia

The Italian section, which focuses on "free time" seen as holidays and the pursuit of nature, is divided into three parts: the past and its unrepeatable "equilibrium for the few" (the harmonious relationship between man and nature); the present and its tumultuous "lost equilibrium" (the multiplication of objects and attitudes; the invasion and destruction of the countryside); and the future or the indication of an "equilibrium to be rediscovered". In the second part, the arrival at the seaside is seen as a moment of joy, an explosion of vitality. The visitor walks down to the sea accompanied by the dynamic perspective of Picasso's figures on a beach that stretches into infinity, towards large, slow-moving waves on rotating rollers.

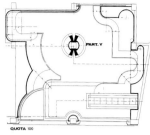

The design of the shop stems from the idea of creating an "Italian piazza." The component elements are the steps, different levels and the continuity of space. This continuity is re-established by the curved surfaces: the geophysical lines that lead back to the concept of the piazza. But the design is dominated by the universe of architecture, using materials offered by modern technology, like laminated plastic and stainless steel. The composition rotates around three fixed points: the steps, an architectural element that symbolizes continuity; the central pillar, correlated to the idea of the capsule, the shape of the future; and Man, represented by the African woodcarving.

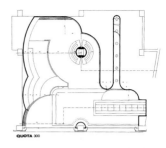

QUOTA 300

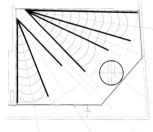

The shop "explodes" around the corner of two streets in the city center. This is the first impression created by the display steps that fan out from inside the space and the mirrors lining the walls and ceiling, multiplying them with a kaleidoscopic effect. The purpose was to create an Olivetti presence in a metropolis like Buenos Aires, with exhibitions of several different objects, small and large machines in a variety of styles by different designers. The pyramid of display shelves is divided by a narrow passage, with a stair leading to a basement office. The aluminium and perspex lamps were specifically designed for this space.

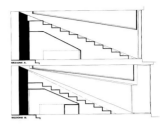

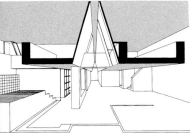

House for an Art Collector, Milan, 1969

with Federico Zürcher
Lighting Design: Livio Castiglioni and Piero Castiglioni

Olivetti Travelling Exhibition
Concept and Form, 1969-1970

Paris, Musée des Arts Decoratifs, Palais du Louvre. Barcelona, Pabellon Italiano de la Feria de Muestras. Madrid, Palacio de Cristal, Parque del Retiro. Edinburgh, Waverley Market Hall. London, Euston Square Station. Tokyo, Prince Hotel Place.

with Federico Zürcher

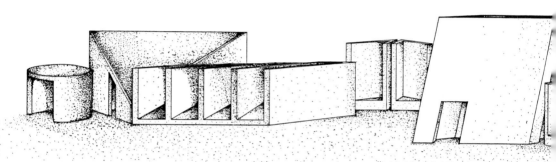

In architectural terms, the exhibition aims to convey the company's experience by describing and recounting the history of its research and choices. The intention is to create a relationship with the visitor in order to evoke a dynamic of reciprocal responsibility. In this sense, the exhibition system can not merely support the material on display, but it also participates, it becomes involved, with the clear intention of involving the spectator. The exhibition is arranged in a sequence that allows the visitor to create his own imaginative, and at the same time instructive, experience.

FIAT Showroom, Zurich, 1970

with Federico Zürcher

The unfair comparison between cars driving along the road and the immobile cars in the closed exhibit space prompted the idea of bringing the road into the showroom. The façade of the building in Zurich was "pushed" inward creating two cages: one is the entrance for the public, and the other, containing a car, is an anomalous car park.

House in Parma, 1975

with Federico Zürcher

The square house, and the long, low wall that adjoins it, mirror the structure of the Emilian landscape, scored by parallel rows of trees and governed by irrigation canals. Built for clients interested in country living, the house is fully equipped to deal with the different seasonal requirements. For the winter, a room with a fireplace acts as the winter extension of the living room and the kitchen, because the fireplace is also used for cooking. For the summer there is a swimming pool, with a pebbled bottom so that the reflections from the water resemble those of a stream. The square roof is supported by four blocks, containing three bedrooms and the room with a fireplace.

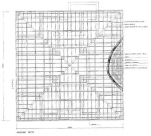

Re-use of Lingotto, Turin, 1983

International invited competition
with Marco Buffoni, Giuseppe Raboni, Italo Rota, Silvana Sermisoni, Takashi Shimura, Chiara Vitali
and with Luca Beltrami Gadola, Luigi Mazza

The underlying theme that inspired the project was its new residential use.

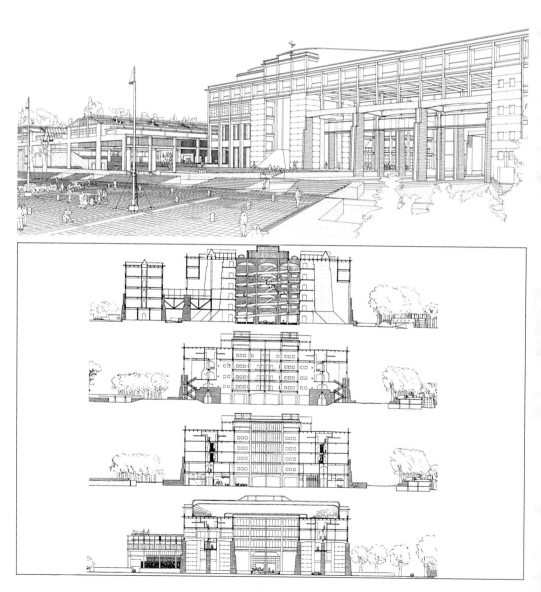

Bicocca Project, Milan, 1986

International invited competition
with Marco Buffoni, Francesca Fenaroli, Laura Peretti, Gabriella Rinaldi, Piero Russi, Takashi Shimura, Chiara Vitali
and with Felice Ippolito, Angelo Lassini, Giorgio Morini, Anna Semenza, Giorgio Spatti

The Pirelli-Breda-Falck industrial zone represented a barrier that has impeded the development of connections with the surrounding urban area. The project aims at retaining the key transversal and longitudinal lines of the current layout, without recreating the closed, monolithic character of the area.

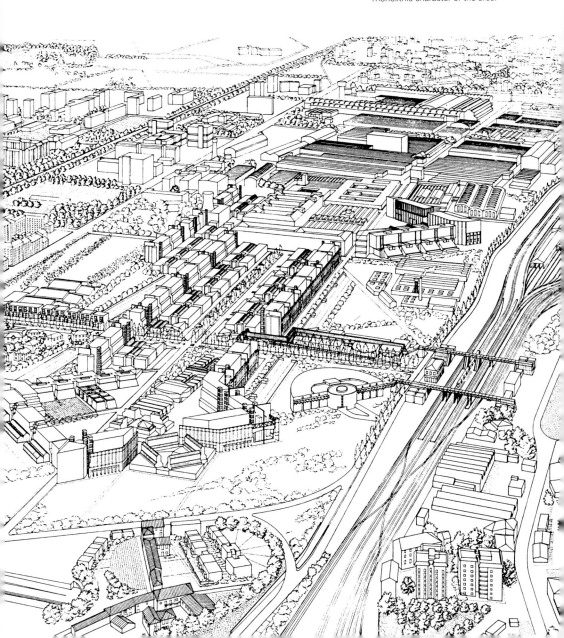

Palazzo Grassi, Venice, 1986
and exhibitions *Futurism and Futurisms*,
1986 and *Balthus*, 2001

Remodelling: with Francesca Fenaroli, Piero Russi and with Antonio Foscari
Exhibition layout: with Francesca Fenaroli
Lighting Design: Piero Castiglioni

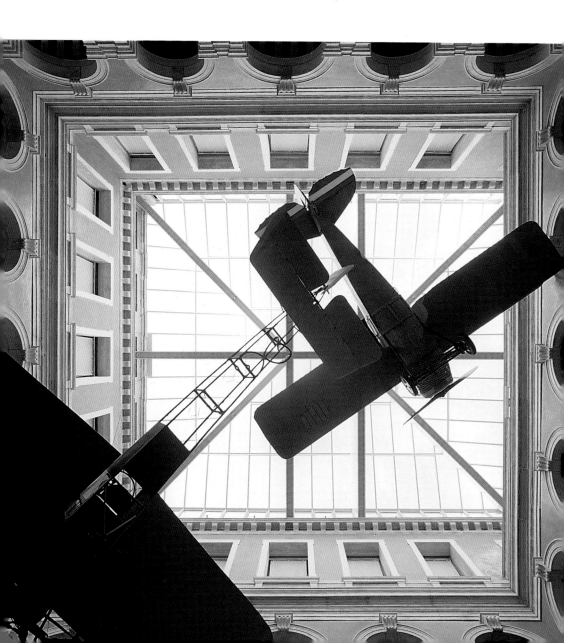

Redesign of the "Salle des Etats", Louvre Museum, Paris, 1991

International invited competition
with Marco Buffoni, Francesca Fenaroli, Vittoria Massa, Raffaella Pirini,
Piero Russi and with Renaud Pierard
Lighting Design: Piero Castiglioni

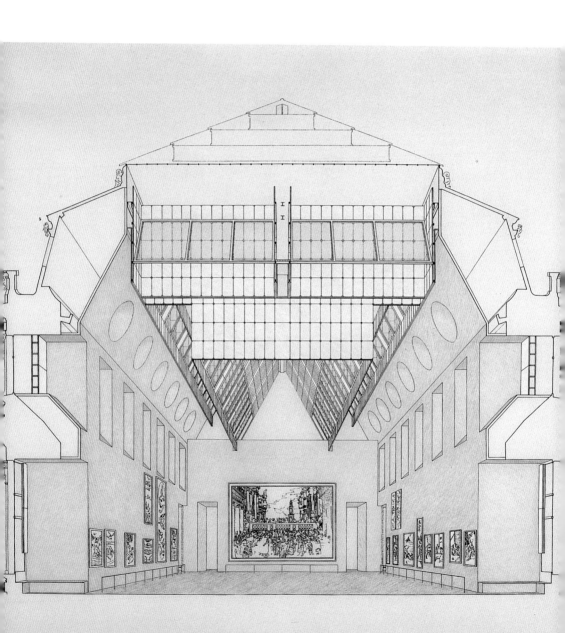

The idea was to give the new room a strong identity by using contemporary language to restore its monumental appearance. Openings down the side walls allow light to be fully controlled. The lower windows were closed to comply with the museum setting, except for the end windows, which are reference elements in the Palace. The glass and alabaster ceiling controls zenithal light, carrying it deep down into the room. *The Marriage at Cana* by Veronese is placed on the northern wall and lit by daylight on both sides, reminiscent of its original position in the refectory of San Giorgio Maggiore. *La Gioconda* is hung on the southern wall completely enclosed in glass.

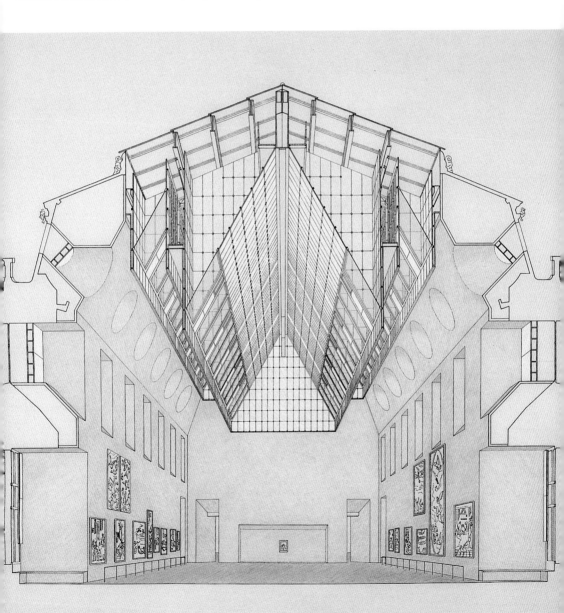

Layout for *The Italian Metamorphosis, 1943-1968* Exhibition, Solomon R. Guggenheim Museum, New York, 1994

with Vittoria Massa and Giovanna Buzzi (costume designer)
Exhibition organization: Germano Celant, Curator of Contemporary Art,
Solomon R. Guggenheim Museum New York

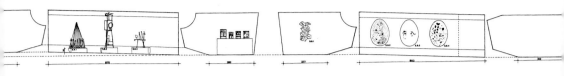

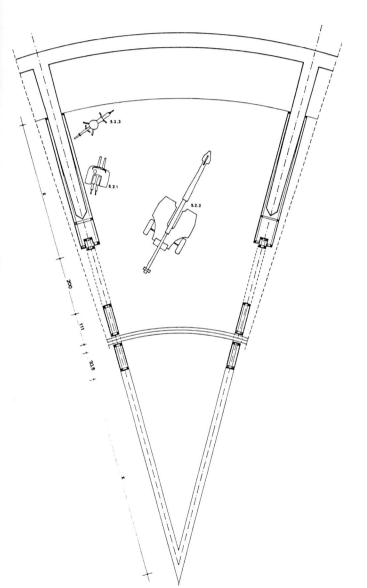

"It took a lot of courage to intevene in the Guggenheim spiral. On arriving in New York, I didn't go immediately to the museum. I preferred to wait another day before seeing the results. The newspapers described it as a challenge to Wright. But I know that I was right in creating a division of opinion. Celant told me that this exhibition should have four strong points, the ones that triggered artistic attitudes. I thought it necessary to say this, in a recognizable, not descriptive way. By generating from the ramp, in the sections devoted to the four artists, rooms only marked by their walls. First I had to break the continuum of the spiral, which makes everything equal. The only way was to project these "rooms" into the space, toward the invisible centre of the museum. But the slope made it necessary to use wedges and the insurance companies prevented us from exhibiting certain works in empty space as we wanted to. Some have screamed at the sacrilege. They are the ones who want untouchable cathedrals. I think that a different reading, above all if it is a temporary one, is enriching. I now know that the Guggenheim is an impossible museum, designed to amaze and not help the visitor. I love Wright and I am attracted by his organic and utopian relationship with the world. But I do not like a museum that is so open, so outstretched towards the infinity. In my opinion, there must always be a beginning and an end."

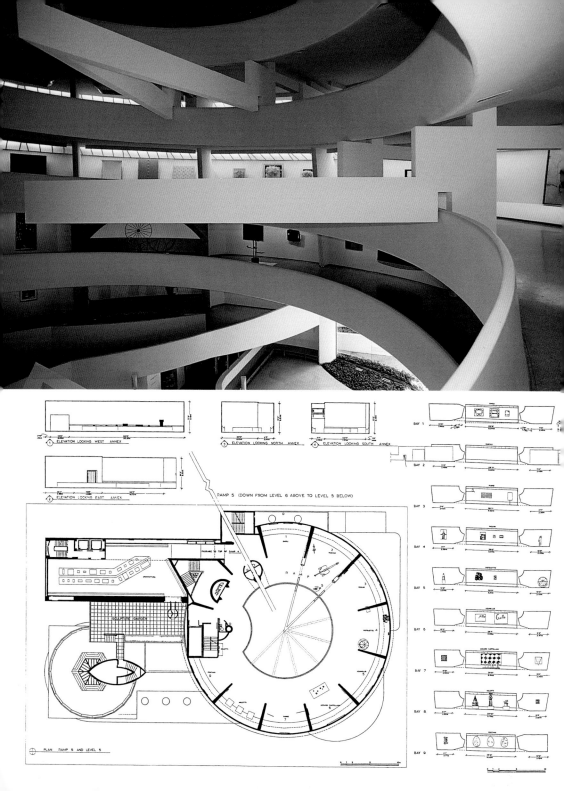

The Italian Metamorphosis, 1943-1968

Temporary Exhibition Gallery
at Milan Triennale, 1994

with Piero Russi
and with Francesco Florulli (Studio GA Architetti Associati)
Lighting Design: Piero Castiglioni

The commission was to study a new gallery to be used to exhibit architectural drawings in view of a specific programme of future exhibitions, as part of the renewal plan for Giovanni Muzio's Palazzo dell'Arte (1933), which houses the Milan Triennale.

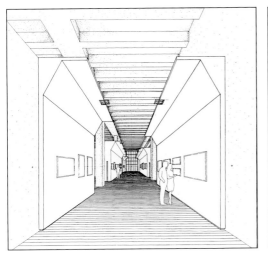
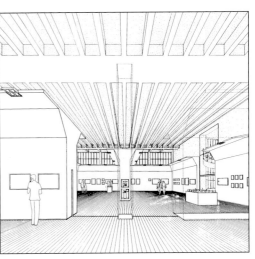
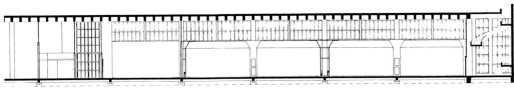

Piazza in front of the former "Leopolda" station, Florence, 1996

with Piero Russi
and with Bianca Ballestrero
Lighting Design: Piero Castiglioni

In view of the reuse of the Leopolda Station, the design for the square creates a space for access and waiting that reproduces outside the structural elements of the internal space. The rhythm produced by the metal columns emphasizes the longitudinal axis and, together with the cross structures, creates the effect of a large pergola.

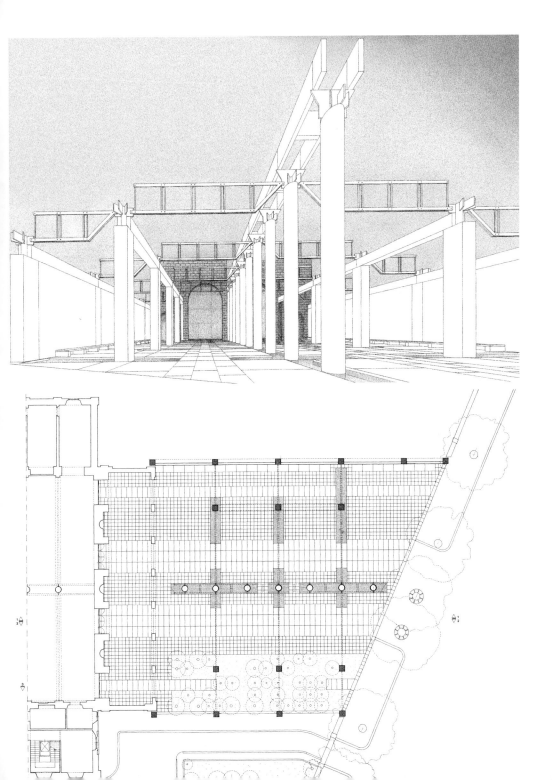

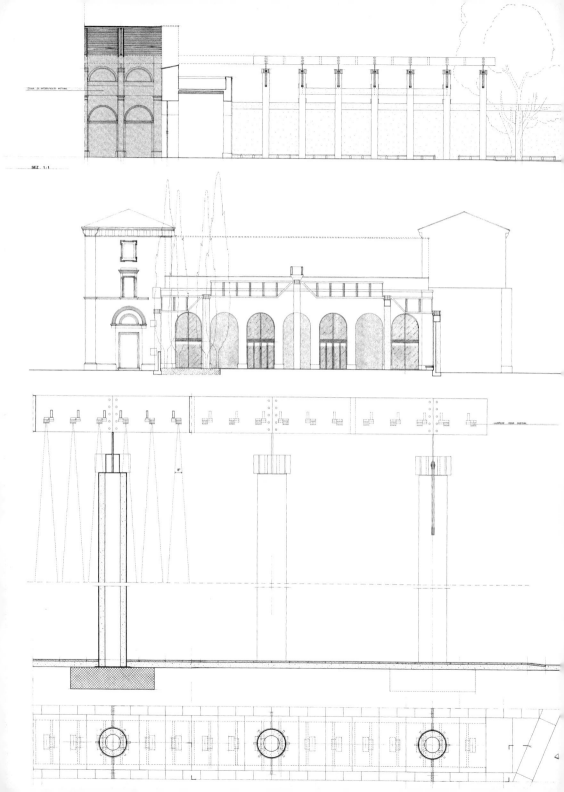

SEZ. 1:1

LAMPADE RDSE DATTIMA

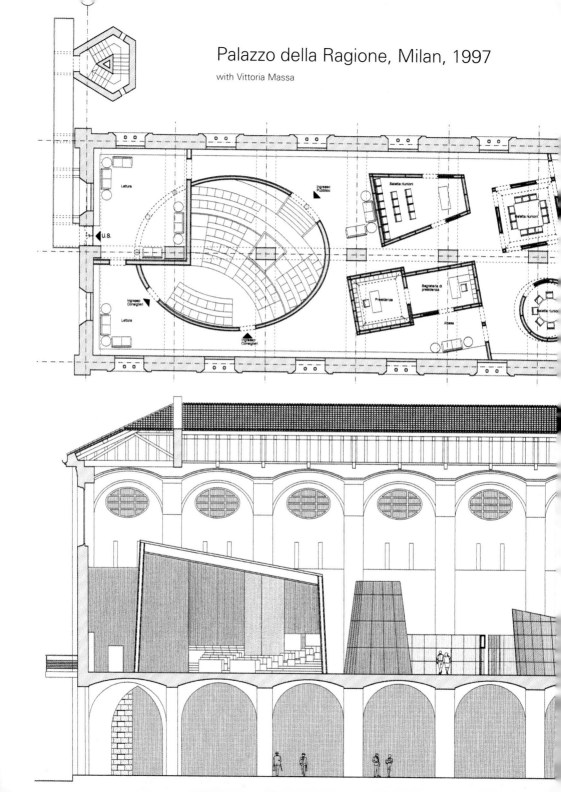

Palazzo della Ragione, Milan, 1997

with Vittoria Massa

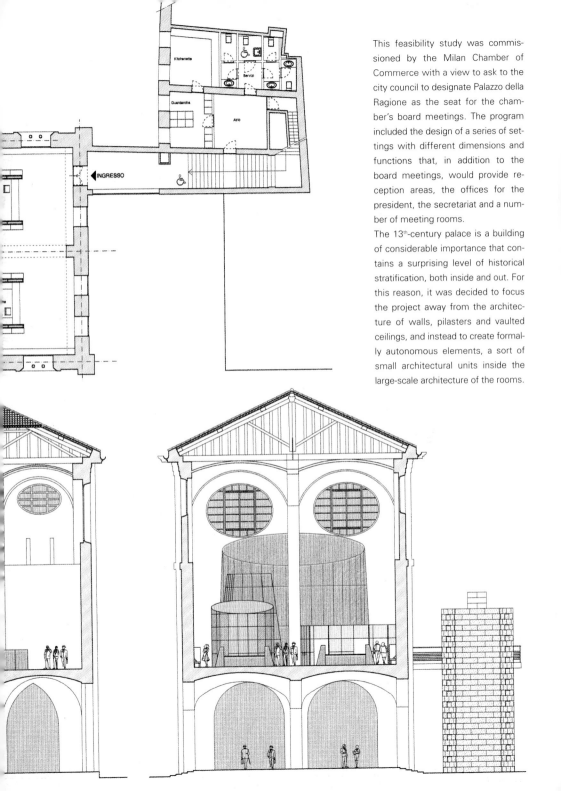

This feasibility study was commissioned by the Milan Chamber of Commerce with a view to ask to the city council to designate Palazzo della Ragione as the seat for the chamber's board meetings. The program included the design of a series of settings with different dimensions and functions that, in addition to the board meetings, would provide reception areas, the offices for the president, the secretariat and a number of meeting rooms.

The 13th-century palace is a building of considerable importance that contains a surprising level of historical stratification, both inside and out. For this reason, it was decided to focus the project away from the architecture of walls, pilasters and vaulted ceilings, and instead to create formally autonomous elements, a sort of small architectural units inside the large-scale architecture of the rooms.

Spazio Oberdan, Milan, 1999

with Carlo Lamperti - Archicat Srl
Lighting Design: Piero Castiglioni

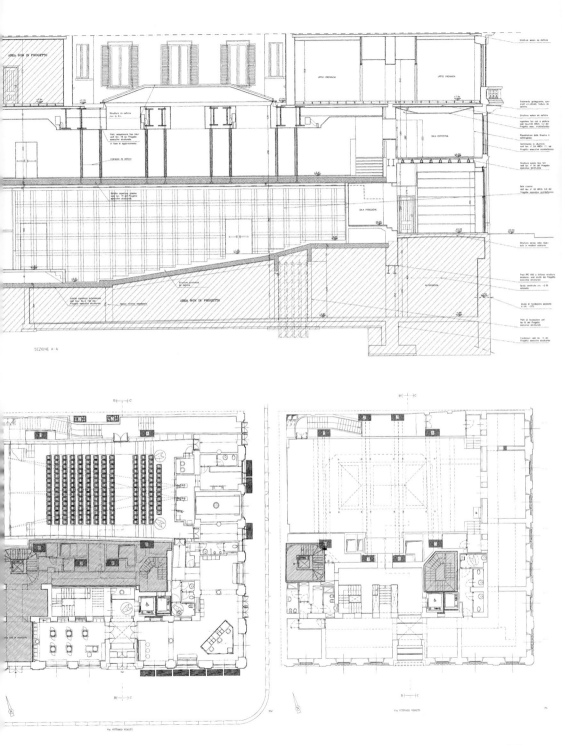

SEZIONE A-A

175

Built at the end of the 19th century, the building that now houses the "Spazio Oberdan" comprised commercial premises on the ground floor and residential apartments on the six upper floors. In the 1930s, rebuilding work for the Giardini Cinema resulted in the courtyard being closed off at the level of the first floor to create the cinema, complete with stalls and a gallery.

The project comprises the ground floor and the first and second storeys. The client's commission was to create a cinema and an exhibition space to be separate, but interconnected and easy to manage. It was decided to use the main en-

trance hall as the access to the multipurpose rooms. Once past the entrance, the small bookshop is on the left and the information center and ticket office for the cinema are on the right. The walls and ceiling of the cinema, seating two hundred, are clad in macoré wood fitted with sound-absorbing panels.

Beyond the entrance, a staircase leads up to the large exhibition room with a floor suspended from the ceiling beams. The exhibition itinerary runs along the two orthogonal sides of the building. On the second floor are the offices used by the Province of Milan.

Former Papal Stables at the Quirinale, Rome, and exhibition *One hundred Impressionist masterpieces from the Hermitage and historical avant-gardes*, 1999

Renovation: with Marco Buffoni
Exhibition layout: with Francesca Fenaroli
Lighting Design: Piero Castiglioni

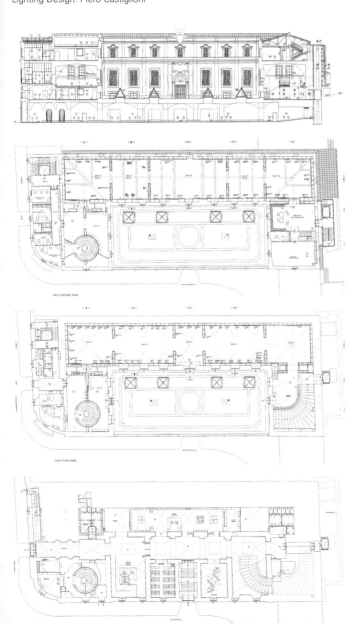

After a public tender, work on the renovation of this magnificent eighteenth-century building was awarded in 1998 and in December 1999 it opened to the public as a new venue for large art exhibitions. Under the supervision of the Superintendence for the Environmental and Architectural Heritage of Rome, the design and subsequent completion of works took less than two years.

"The prime characteristic of the *Scuderie del Quirinale* is their spatial quality, and this had to be retained. What matters, is to understand the differences in order to preserve them. You can find a solution to the dilemma of the museum and the historic building by integrating their different requirements: one must be defended because of its expressive potential, the other must be fitted with services turned into architecture for the exhibition. But the overall intervention should fade compared with the importance of preserving the ability to recognize the place, being invisible as a work and making way for the exhibits on display.

At the *Scuderie* it was important to preserve the existing spatial qualities, because this is the prime feature of this building. The feeling of space is obvious right away on the ground floor, which features the long gallery and the ramp that have both been conserved. The same is true of the upper floors, where minimalist interventions were required, enough to create the surfaces to hang the works."

Wholesale fruit, vegetable and flower market, Genova-Bolzaneto, 1999

European competition open to restricted participants, second phase
with Vittoria Massa
and with Metropolitana Milanese SpA, Giuseppe Boschi, Marco Sibani, Ugo
Maione, Ambiente Italia Srl, SO.GE.MI SpA

The project was based on the functional evidence of the structures that would guarantee flexibility for the stalls. The key feature of the complex, best visible from above, is the architectural solution used for the roof, with a large central skylight that lights and ventilates the entire gallery.

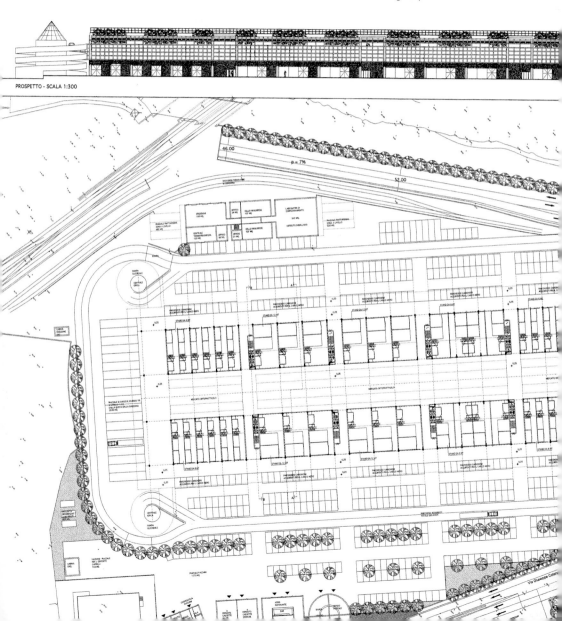

PROSPETTO - SCALA 1:300

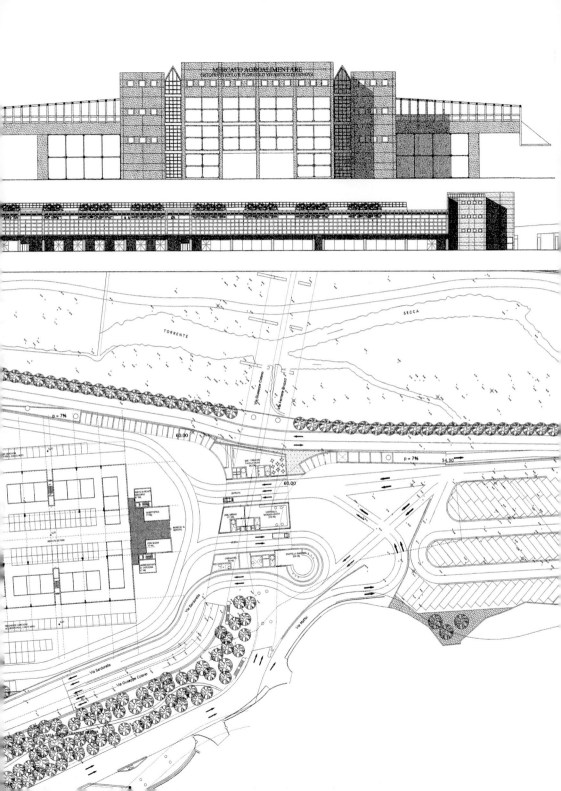

A2 Chiasso-San Gottardo Highway Noise prevention in Bissone-Melide zone, 1999

International competition
with Marco Buffoni, Massimiliano Caruso, Chiaro Costa
and with Marco Marcionelli, Ernst Winkler + Partner AG, Bellinzona

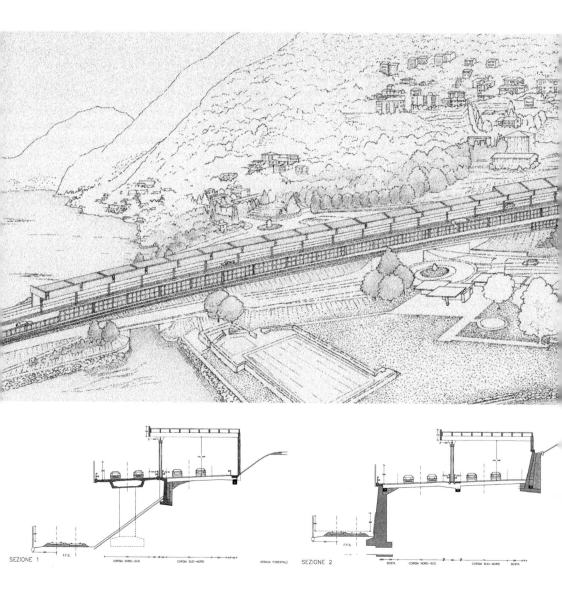

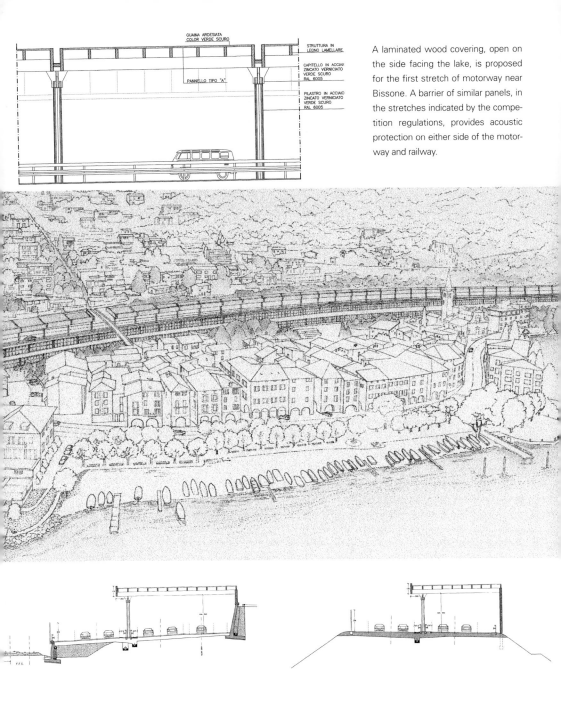

GUAINA ARDESIATA
COLOR VERDE SCURO

STRUTTURA IN
LEGNO LAMELLARE

CAPITELLO IN ACCIAI
ZINCATO VERNICIATO
VERDE SCURO
RAL 6005

PANNELLO TIPO "A"

PILASTRO IN ACCIAIO
ZINCATO VERNICIATO
VERDE SCURO
RAL 6005

A laminated wood covering, open on the side facing the lake, is proposed for the first stretch of motorway near Bissone. A barrier of similar panels, in the stretches indicated by the competition regulations, provides acoustic protection on either side of the motorway and railway.

SEZIONE 5

SOSTA   CORSIA NORD–SUD   CORSIA SUD–NORD   USCITA   SOSTA

BANCHINA DI EMERGENZA   CORSIA NORD–SUD   CORSIA SUD–NORD   BANCHINA DI EMERGENZA

4

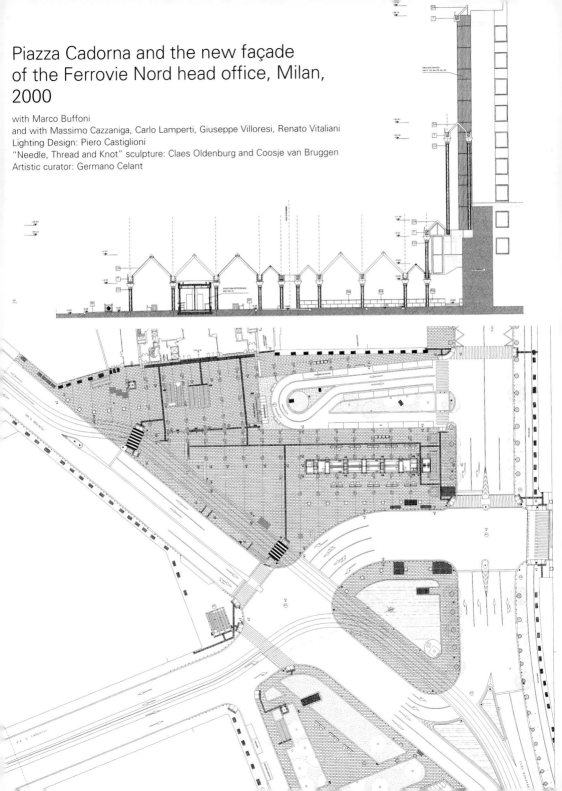

Piazza Cadorna and the new façade
of the Ferrovie Nord head office, Milan,
2000

with Marco Buffoni
and with Massimo Cazzaniga, Carlo Lamperti, Giuseppe Villoresi, Renato Vitaliani
Lighting Design: Piero Castiglioni
"Needle, Thread and Knot" sculpture: Claes Oldenburg and Coosje van Bruggen
Artistic curator: Germano Celant

The aim of the project was to restore the square's lost role as a public place by rationalizing the traffic flow and designing a space for pedestrian use and transit, partially covered by a colonnaded structure in aluminium and glass that rises up to complete the façade of the Ferrovie Nord.

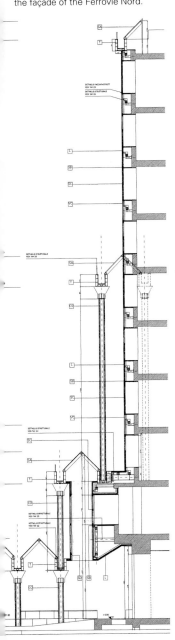

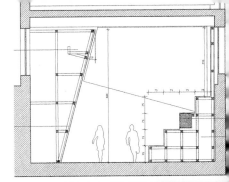

1951-2001 Made in Italy?
Exhibition, Section "Memory,"
Milan Triennale, 2001

with Vittoria Massa, Milena Archetti, Chiara Costa
"Sails" design: Carola Reverdini

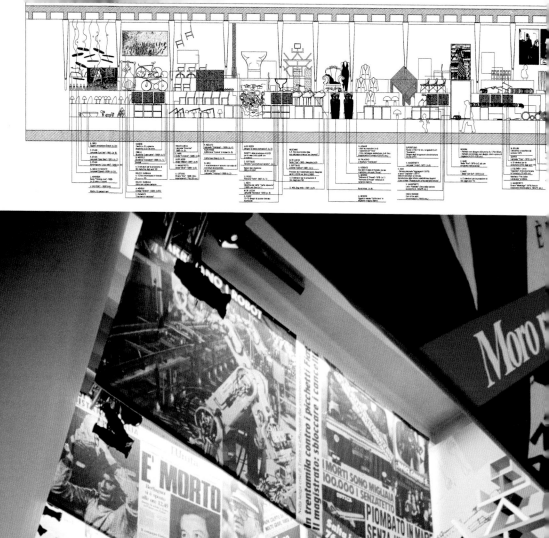

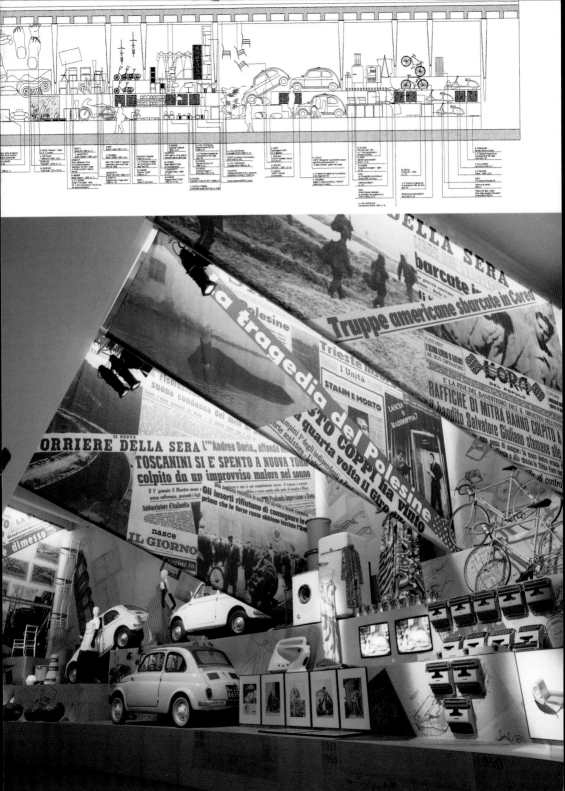

Museo dell'Opera del Duomo, Florence, 2002

International invited competition
with Vittoria Massa

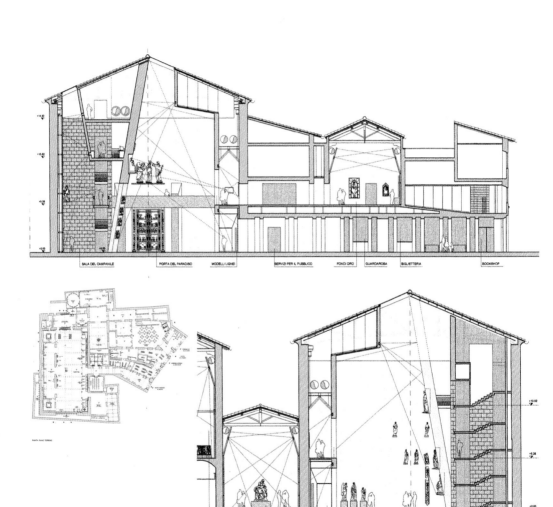

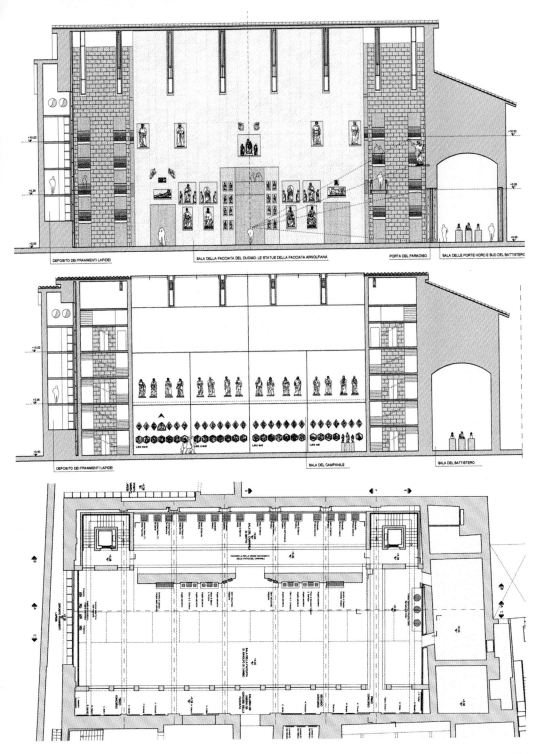

The competition regulations for the extension of the Museo dell'Opera del Duomo, after the acquisition of the building that formerly housed the Teatro degli Intrepidi, stated that projects should:

– Link the new spaces with the recently renovated spaces of the existing museum in a single itinerary, offering a unified concept that would respect the architectural features of the two different spatial units;

– Enhance the value of the exhibition complex, within this single itinerary, remarking the two major sections of the collection: on the one hand, the works that once decorated the exterior of the buildings in Piazza del Duomo, and on the other, the works of art from the interior and the sacred furnishings;

– Make this choice clear so that visitors can correlate the works to their original context;

– Allow for two separate itineraries: a fast track one and an itinerary that would encompass the entire collection;

– Rethink the visitor reception areas for the museum in view of the new itinerary and the increased number of visitors.

The competition offered an opportunity to reflect on the correct placement of sculptures, conceived as monumental features to be viewed from below in public squares. Isolating the masterpieces in the collection was the easiest solution, but not the most effective way of highlighting their value, which is based not only on their exceptional quality but also on the extraordinary concentration of items.

Both natural and artificial lighting play extremely important roles, including zenithal lighting, aiming at recreating the lighting conditions for which the works were conceived.

ANALOGOUS
OBJECTS

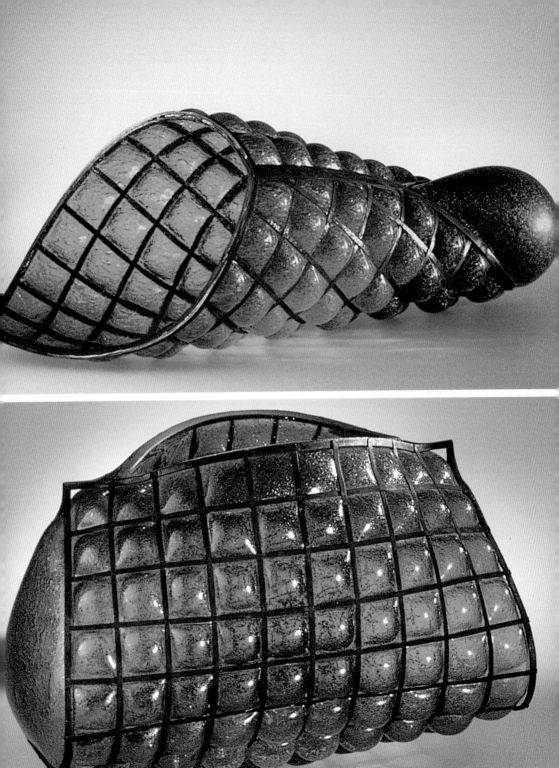

Pipistrello lamp, 1965
Ruspa lamp, 1967
for Martinelli Luce SpA

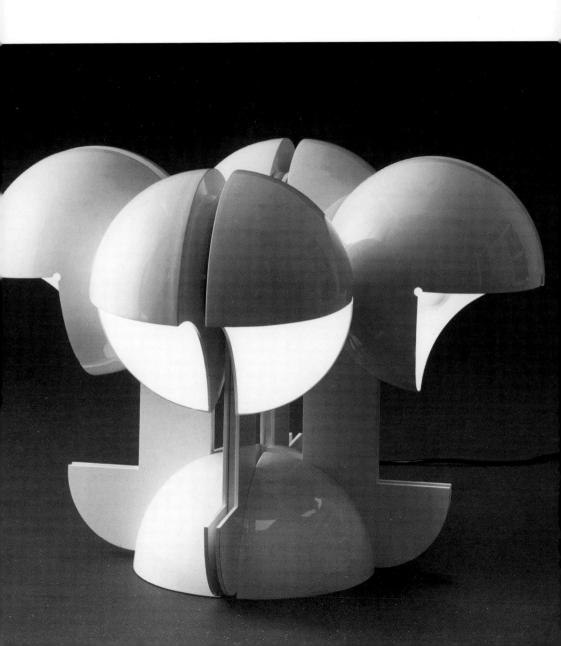

Oracolo and *Mezzoracolo* lamps, 1968
Tennis furniture series, 1971

Oracolo and *Mezzoracolo* for Artemide SpA
Tennis for Knoll International

Locus Solus furniture series, 1964
Sgarsul rocking chair, 1962

Locus Solus for Poltronova Srl (1964), for Zanotta SpA (from 1965)
Sgarsul for Poltronova Srl

King Sun lamp, 1967
Rimorchiatore lamp, 1967
Giova lamp, 1964

King Sun for Kartell SpA
Rimorchiatore for Candle (1967), for Fontana Arte (from 1993);
Giova for Fontana Arte

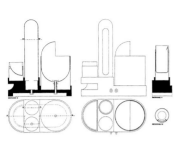

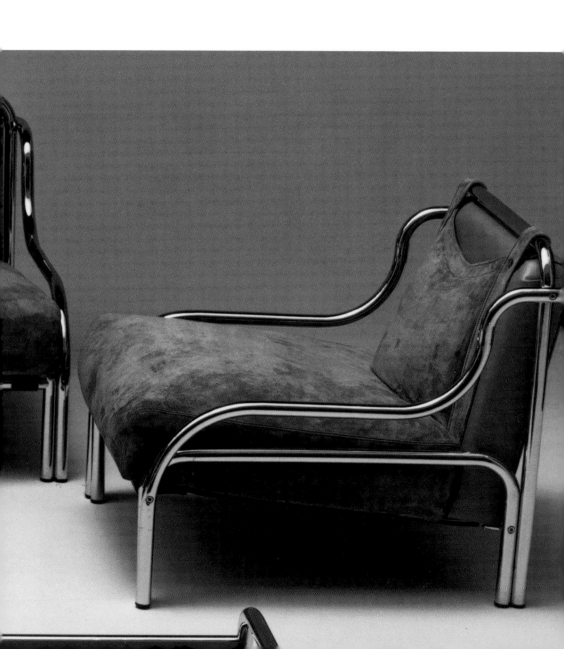

Parola lamp series, 1980

with Piero Castiglioni

for Fontana Arte

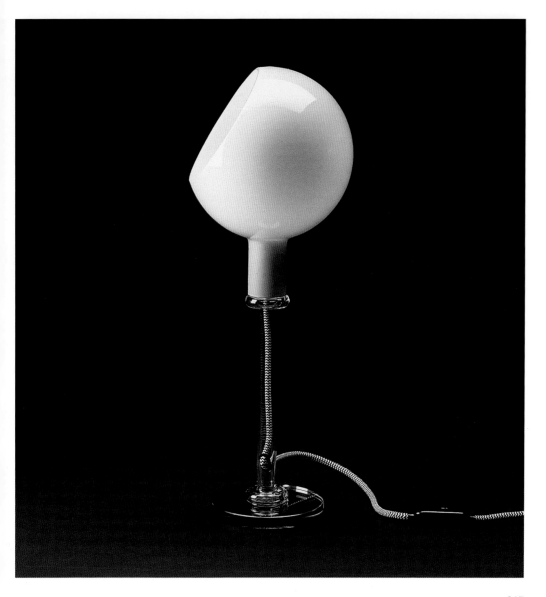

Aprilina chair, 1964
April armchair, 1971

for Zanotta SpA

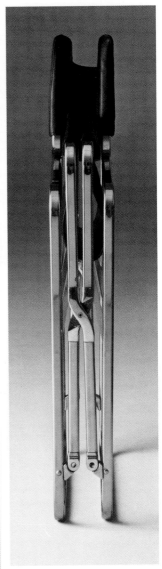

Nina lamp, 1981
Pietra lamp, 1988
Jumbo table, 1965

Nina for Fontana Arte
Pietra for Fontana Arte
Jumbo for Knoll International

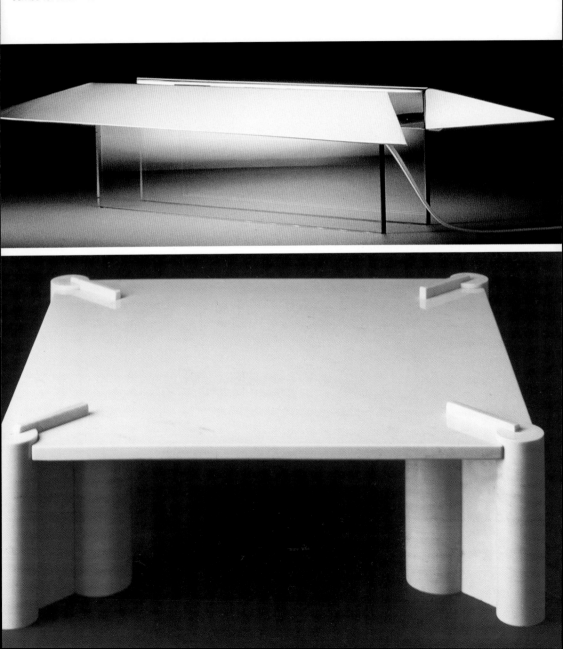

Series of plastic furniture, 1968

Gae Aulenti collection for Kartell SpA

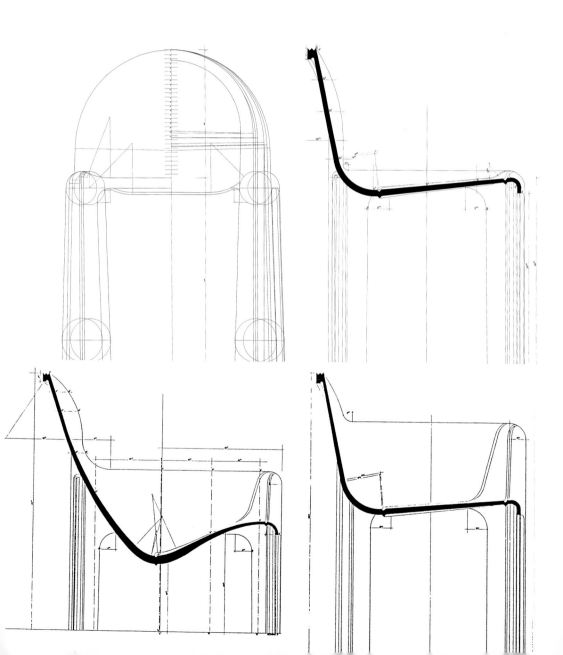

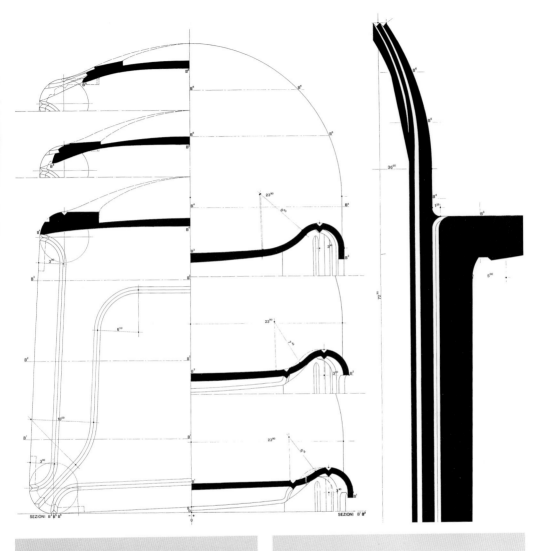

SEZIONI B⁵ B⁶ B⁸   SEZIONI B⁷ B²

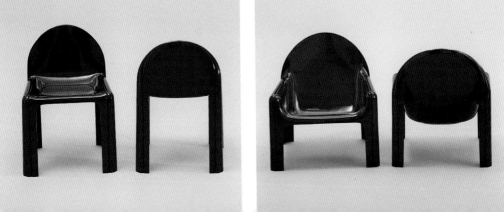

Tour, crystal table
with bicycle wheels, 1993
Crystal table with wheels, 1980

for Fontana Arte

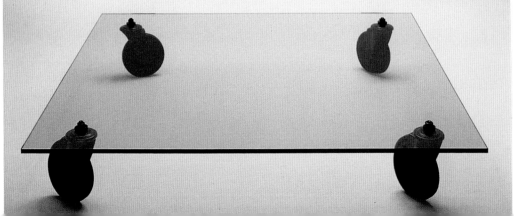

Italy: The New Domestic Landscape,
exhibition at the Museum of Modern Art,
New York, 1972

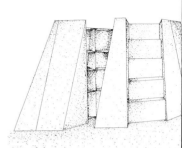

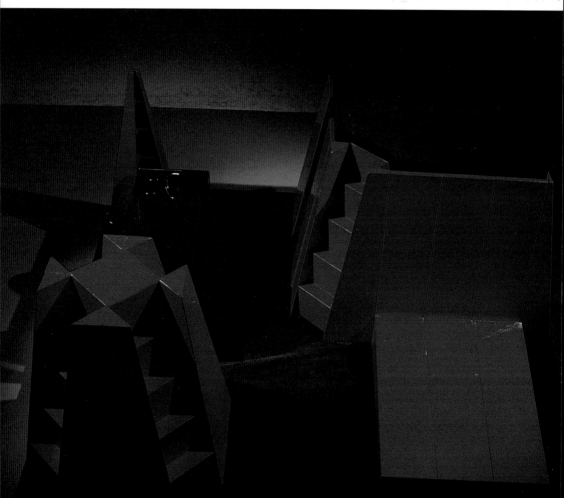

COMMENTARIES

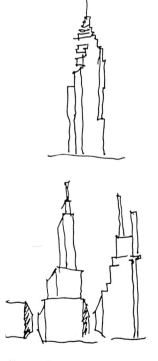

Above and next page:
Preliminary studies for Sakuraokacho Hotel-Office Building in Tokyo, international invited competition, 1992

Commentaries-Correspondence
by Margherita Petranzan

"Critique is concerned with truth content of a work of art, the commentary with its subject matter."

W. Benjamin, *Angelus Novus*

Architecture and history

Back to words again.

Words about things, words that construct, that do without chatter; carefully pondered words, words as heavy as stone, words that argue and ask questions.

In order to "talk" about architectural "things," we must "think" of them as "allegories;" they become true, and they represent and embody the thought that has expressed them "in another way."

Like allegorical forms, architectural forms organize themselves to refer their *raison d'être* to something else. This must be sought through careful analysis in a sum of intents and designs that belong both macroscopically and microscopically to the conceptual structure of the time that has witnessed and allowed their concrete embodiment.

The design of the thing should be sought in its real meaning, in the thought of the period to which it belongs, from which the creator "draws" and "receives" his *raison d'être*, both as a man and as a designer. The thought of the time "designs" the thing, it moulds the work and "decides" its destiny.

The author is the conscious executor and, for this reason, "responsible:" his responsibility only commences because of his awareness of belonging to a complex, multifaceted operating machine that enables his actions, making every "creative urge" instrumental to its growth and "progress."

Although there is no real control, there is a mechanism that, by bringing all the contradictions into play, foresees the emergence of those exceptional traits required to give recognition and breadth to the historical moment that "contains" them.

Dear Gae, your architecture fully expresses the time to which it belongs; however, I would risk calling it "eclectic," if by eclecticism we mean the capacity to choose (derived from the

Greek *eklekticós*, *"the person who chooses"*). In the *"micro-cosms"* of your projects, which normally seem to belong more to the functionalist tradition (linked to the beginnings of the modern movement), reference is undoubtedly made to the os-cillations between modernity and tradition that strongly charac-terized the architectural output of the last century. This can be seen in the way you *"resolved"* the relationship with the *"his-torically structured"* buildings you were asked to *"re-structure."* I am thinking, for example, of the National Museum of Catalan Art in Barcelona in 1985, and the Asian Art Museum of San Francisco in 1996, in which the theme of functional *"modifica-tion"* seems to have been the one you found most challenging.

In San Francisco, for example, you had to do with the city's historic role, the last Western outpost on the Pacific Ocean and the entry point for Asian influence in America, as you had to in-sert your project in an ambitious plan to upgrade the Civic Cen-ter, the heart of official San Francisco and the seat of political and cultural institutions. This is also the area most densely im-bued with history, even if it is relatively recent history, because the city was virtually destroyed by the 1906 earthquake, and the only remnants are the stone buildings of the Civic Center which are regarded as a precious historical heritage. I believe the most important innovation in San Francisco compared to the Musée d'Orsay was having to correlate a building from the European school with a collection of Asian art, even if exten-sive analogies are present because they are both from the Beaux-Arts period. You said, and I agree, that one of the most urgent problems concerned the transformation from a building used as a library, with static functions (people sit down in a li-brary), into a building with dynamic functions, like a museum, which invites the visitor to walk through it. Sufficient light and air, an easy orientation, the best possible perception of art-works with no obstacles, were some of the essential aspects of the new functional layout. I am also convinced that in this case the relationship with the historical *"memories"* of the var-ious civilizations exhibited inside the same building was essen-tial to resolve the project. The result is radically different from what you might have imagined in a city not heavily influenced by the presence and co-existence of different ethnic groups, like San Francisco where every ethnic community is jealously protective of its past, in spite of all feeling profoundly Ameri-

"The building to be transformed, to be reused, is seen as a contemporary entity. That is to say that I feel that one of the constants is the place of foundation, the existing building as it is and its relationship with the museological program. The other constant is the problem of the function of the museum that is being built, and this has to be seen as contemporary. Then, too, there is the problem of the new architecture, which cannot be subjected to the architecture of the existing building even though it derives from it."

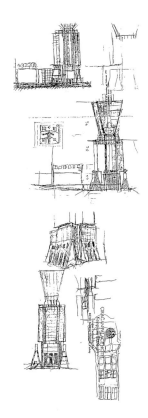

can. For you the challenge of the "new" (San Francisco - Barcelona - Paris - New York) therefore involves all these elements, which intervene together as continuous and necessary linguistic "interferences," and consists in a sort of ethical regulatory principle in a "game" where the rules are fixed by the infinite variables you have managed to identify, with painstaking precision, in every place where you have been asked to intervene.

In his "theses on the philosophy of history," Benjamin affirms that "the true picture of the past flits by" and that "to articulate the past historically does not mean to recognize it the way it really was; it means to seize hold of a memory as it flashes up in a moment of danger."

I believe that this historical moment is unravelling between dangers and contradictions and that the contemporary inclusion of all the "applicative" possibilities gives rise to blinding flashes, certainly not illuminations regarding the past and much less the future of the human agglomerates known as cities. The city is and always will be a contemporary series of events, a complex system of relationships that intersect at different levels, an ongoing process involving the transformation of reality that must be understood using different disciplines and technically sophisticated instruments because the city is both Babylon and Jerusalem, always antagonists but co-existing. The two cities, Babylon or confusion, Jerusalem or vision of peace, have been merged together since the origins of mankind itself and will continue until the end of time.

The city is therefore the necessary and contemporary implementation of all the contradictions; it is that common place, in the literary sense of the term, where the insoluble conflict between good and evil is staged, the place where the universe of the possible is organized, which is both reality and fiction, the real world and the fairy tale.

The city is an urbanized territory, but also the set of people who inhabit it. But what is the relationship today between the city of objects and the city of men?

I believe that in our present age—which is anything but "Messianic"—the relations between men and things form part of two worlds: one which is apparently real and another genuinely apparent. These alternate dangerously on the horizon of

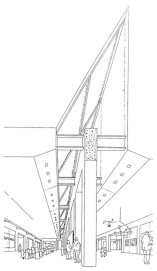

Aragon Museum of Contemporary Art in Saragoza
International invited competition, 1993
Perspective section of the gallery

every refounding project. For this reason, the "construction" of any value assumes different properties depending on its inclusion in one or other world; therefore what happens is only justified *a posteriori* with the considerable risk that the implosion of reality into concrete fact eliminates the possibility of abstracting from it, given that it is already presented as a total abstraction: in other words, the fact "happens," without first being thought, it "lacks" any form of historic memory.

Dear Gae, on the subject of "commonplaces," I would like to recall the adventure that we shared in the competition-tender for the Fenice Theater. What I remember with great pleasure is the moment of starting work, namely the most complex phase, during which we attempted to give a rigorous historical and critical justification to all our actions, although we were by definition constrained by the dictates of "where it was and how it was" laid down by the regulations. I won't dwell on the fact that after eight months of work in progress, our contract was annulled following an appeal resulting from procedural errors made by the awarding body; instead, I believe that on that occasion, I was able to understand and get to know the tone of your design methodology, which is very different from my own but certainly worthy of respectful recognition. The patient work of analysis and the re-composition of all the elements belonging to the project on which you, in that instance, had embarked, made me understand that, for you, nothing can be left to improvisation and, above all, that your knowledge of the subject forms part of the "thing" you are doing: it is a sort of diachronic and controlled application of different forms of knowledge. I think I can affirm that, while always remaining faithful to those thoughts clearly generated by the observation of objects, you successfully changed and converted them into architecture.

One can also say that the city represents a "necessary" recovery of memory and rooting in it, but it also represents experimentation and projection into the future through the construction of the present.

Alberti states that in order to accomplish a real innovation, the "veteres" must become the "nos", and for this reason, they cease, by definition, to be "ancient", thus renouncing

"Sometimes people speak about reality as if a field effectively existed where it is expressed. Instead, there are infinite realities."

"In my opinion, culture is subject to only one thing: production. The consumption of culture cannot exist by definition. Otherwise, it would be immobilized. This is contrary to its very definition."

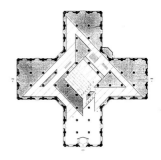

Installation for the "Christo" exhibit, Rotonda della Besana, Milan, 1973 Plan

their identification. The new building betrays the values on which it is founded and which belong to tradition only because it "must" assume and appropriate them. When this does not happen, the act of building falls prey to the most fortuitous and horrendous individual will. Precepts, measurements and authentic relations with the stratifications of time are laid down and can be read in works of architecture that always and under all circumstances represent the period that produced them. Without exception, every building contributes to the formation of the city, on whose image rests the credibility of the human structure that built it. Contrary to other arts, architecture is representative; it is conditioned by and conditions reality, which through its "image" is "clothed" with meaning. It conditions reality because it gives reality a form that becomes its irreplaceable expression and limit, its measurement. But it is also conditioned by reality because it intervenes inside what has already been built which absorbs and often irremediably swallows up the new project, in particular when the only canons of reference and insertion are the horrendous breakdown brought about by the territorial planning of contemporary society. Therefore, should we view the city as a quantitative assembling of buildings whose basic function is to "contain" the disaster towards which the human condition is heading? Is the contemporary city, with its striking "absence" of architecture, perhaps not a mirror of the diaspora of values that resist unification, a humanity that can no longer learn the art of living through constant exercise and training of self, through self: that authentic *askèsis*, the exercise of thought on oneself which reactivates what one knows, preparing oneself to face reality?

In this type of city, the fruit of the systematic discharge from self, of dispersion, excess and fragmentation (of reading, writing, signs and words) can there still be room (physically and mentally) for architectural constructions that communicate and represent values on which and for which they should be built?

Architecture and politics

We can still state that the city is the sum of overlapping services, but it is also the structure that manages and runs them; what is this, if not the form of city government? And what does city government consist of now, or rather what should it con-

Project for the Perugia Business Centre, international competition, 1971
Perspective

sist of in this manifest disintegration and destruction? How can there be an authoritative government in a city built in disintegrated and chaotic parts?

The contemporary city has become a redundant phenomenon; it is a large mutant form, with times and methods that differ significantly from previous centuries. Until a few decades ago, decentralization was seen as a solution because it contained the germs of a utopia that would create another new city, different from the existing one, in which to implement social justice and, by rebuilding the system of relations, to regenerate the institutions and their government. Nowadays, having ascertained the failure of decentralization, the city is exploding and imploding at the same time. Explosion transforms the condition of staying into that of traversing, and implosion turns every individual into a drifting mine given that he or she has inwardly absorbed all the contradictions present outside what I like to define as the "destructive condition" of contemporary construction. Can one perhaps venture to say that this type of city, which can no longer be *seen* in its entirety, and consequently whose development can no longer be controlled, because every object and every place is a city, is a mental condition, that it is a "spirit-city" as well as a "world-city," and that its physical nature consists in the only form of reality, namely that of the means of communication?

I believe that the city generates both the production and organization of work, but also the equal distribution of the latter; but what values does work have today?

By multiplying itself, the division of labor has produced the merciless objectivity of every human relationship filtered by money and the exchange of goods. Precision, security and certainty in formal conventions ruled by clocks have been introduced into relations between the elements of existence, by the essence of money, which is calculation. Moreover, given that working relations increasingly reflect this complexity and multiplicity, they become more impersonal and immersed in rigid schemes requiring the division of roles and obliging the individual to carry out increasingly segmented activities, whose extreme forms all too often lead to the impoverishment of the personality as a whole. I think that I can venture a paradox, which I would term a paradox of reality, or of freedom: as a man-world, the citizen immersed in the objective civilization of

"As architecture is gradually excluded from the contamination of the world, it becomes hardened in its rules because when you are rejected, you attack."

"Any human object, be it a monument or a den, cannot escape its relationship with the city, the place that represents the human condition."

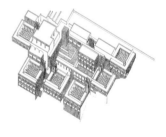

Project for a residential complex in Caracas, 1978
Axonometry

233

the metropolis, experiences complete freedom to be completely restricted.

From such destruction, can we restore any meaning to individual work?

Perhaps this can still be done through responsible reference to a sense of belonging, to a purpose?

But what form should all this take at an institutional level?

The uprooting, loss of place and the lack of identity of mass-man are apparently recomposed and annulled precisely in the type of residential developments found in the vast peripheral areas of contemporary cities, typologies that restore today's preferred dimension in an abstract manner: the consumption of the dream; a dream during the sleep of reason, one that continues to produce monsters and always will.

What do the concepts of internationalizm and localizm mean in this context?

Perhaps we must go beyond the multiple meanings, recognizing the difference between various specific moments and, through this recognition, learn to distinguish, make evaluations, and ask ourselves questions that will lead to change.

Dear Gae, by working in different cities, metropolises or megalopolises in what is now a globalized world, your position in relation to the "governments" of the places where you work must be problematic or, at least, difficult to manage on each occasion. For example, when you designed the new layout for Piazzale Cadorna and the new façade for the Ferrovie Nord, a project containing a "strong sign," difficult to be accepted, or the reorganization of the square in front of the former Leopolda station, about which the same can also be said, I imagine that relations with the local authorities and the bureaucratic structures that "oversee" our work, mortifying it by reducing it to the banal application of regulations that are slavishly transformed into forms, were complex to say the least.

In an interview with "La Repubblica" on 4 November 2000, talking about San Francisco and the United States, you declared that, as a European, you were passionately excited by the fact that they represent a crossroads of civilizations, where several cultures can live side by side without relinquishing their separate identities, and that as an Italian, you were amazed (given that it doesn't happen in Italy) and full of admiration for a

Studies for the *Parola* lamp, 1980

country where major works are approved, funded and completed with such speed. I would like to dwell for a moment on what you described as your extraordinary experience in Paris working on the old Gare d'Orsay, now transformed into a museum. Among the architects that must have fascinated you, I think one must have been a Mannerist, basically because of the calibrated balance between symmetry and asymmetry, continuity and discontinuity, that I perceived the moment I visited your "calligraphic" intervention. The fact that you succeeded in blending forms belonging to totally different functions in a city that normally undertakes the most unthinkable formal risks and the most futuristic design experiments solely to "display" the political and economic power of the historical period that created them, led me to infer that your relations with the administration and the bureaucratic structure must have been much less burdensome in this case.

But in the today's diaspora of buildings, in the total city or world-city, whatever you wish to call it, at this devastated historic moment, when the emergence of all the unweighed contradictions controlled by ideologies inevitably descends into religious fundamentalisms, I believe that it is vital to give "political" reasons to an action (architectural discipline) that, paradoxically, after such a long time, finds itself for the very first time inside a political "vacuum," in the sense that it is not directly connected to it. It is terrible but true: I am convinced that because we are experiencing a worldwide lack of opposed forms of political "ideologies," there may be an increase in conflict between peoples, but this will not have immediate repercussions on architecture, which is going "adrift:" beeing at the mercy of dangerous and unbridled artistic and economic "personalisms."

However, what has dramatically changed, I believe, also in architecture, after the massacre in New York of September 11th, is that the terrible gesture which, in an instant, wiped out an urban history that was highly representative of the affirmation of the International Style, was the macabre product of a young Egyptian architect, Mohammed Atta, born into that westernised Arab middle class that has helped to swell the ranks of the "global" and multiethnic bourgeoisie that for several decades now has determined the face and the "form" of cities, metropolises and megalopolises.

"A problem that must always be kept in mind when designing museums and art galleries is that of the visitors. I feel that the act of visiting a museum represents real work for each age and for each specialization."

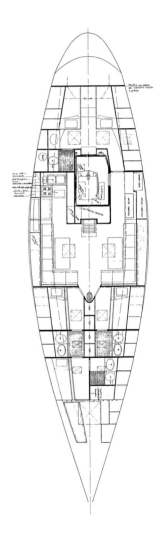

Interior design for a sailing boat, 1986
Plan

More than ever before, architects and politicians should now collaborate to provide an answer, no longer and not only in terms of planning control, but rather for built space in which to live in a civilized manner in the complexity of the modern diffused city; the absence of political leadership has undermined the foundations shared by several cultures for a theory of architecture that forms part, the world over, of the same capitalization that governs all goods.

Architecture and technique

The vacuum of politics, now transformed into techno-politics, is alarming and has given rise to the extraordinary need to rethink a new concept of "political," because we are living in a time of destructive "transitions." The political dimension cannot be relegated to the limbo between the excessive power of technology, which tends to monopolize decisions, and religion which is increasingly filled with sense and charged, in symbolic terms worldwide, with values that are highly representative of the human condition and the protest underlying the legitimate vindication of rights. I believe the only way of opposing a general uniformity and adaptation solely at an infrastructural level (not affirming, as many architects risk doing, that form is dead and irrelevant) is the critical approach, also through form, which undoubtedly cannot solve our social problems immediately (as Le Corbusier thought it would), but it can play a "critical" role by asking what it is correct or important to be done now. I believe that architecture is not the immediate conductor of values and content, but that, potentially, form can "generate" values and point to new contents (for example, the design for a new museum does not embody and does not itself contain meaning, as in the past, but it can certainly generate the possibility of another way of intending museums), although within today's rapidly spreading deconstructivism, all forms interact with the forms themselves, not with the contents. Therefore, in my opinion, the form of architecture, which does not mean the search for new styles, must also withstand the "simplifications" typical of "contemporaneousness", aimed at deconstruction for its own sake. However, this resistance must push beyond the set limits, following the example set by the great architects of all time, from Brunelleschi to Loos and Mies.

It is not a question of style, but of method and the ability to

Villa in Parma, 1975
Axonometry

capture at a precise moment the right way to oppose the standardization of customs and consumption; I believe it is also important to resist consumption of the image of architecture, because this represents both space and time; every individual work has its own identity because it can resist different kinds of repression. "I see the form that had come to life before my eyes vanishing, the form that made each phenomenon unique, and a singular emptying of reality turns men and objects into larvae" (Romano Guardini). The "emptying of reality" that Guardini writes of with extraordinary foresight—in letters written in 1927 that were recovered by Mies van der Rohe—is now completely under the sway of technology and its power.

Dear Gae, I want to underline your rigorous technical and scientific approach toward the architectures you construct, every time that you design. As Vitruvius said, for you architecture is above all a science, even if it is "adorned"—or better "equipped" with other disciplines. In this respect, I think that one of your last sites, the museum in San Francisco, is even surprising in technological terms because you are completely rebuilding the foundations. Each steel pier that supported the old building has been shored up and suspended. The new load-bearing structure stands on enormous "base isolators" of steel and rubber, because you told me that, in the event of an earthquake, given that it has no natural anti-seismic elasticity, a large stone building needs to be anchored at the bottom and constrained at the top; moreover, the ability to load foundation piers on isolators is a technological miracle because it allows the building to swing up to one and a half meters. I mention this example to show that each of your projects has the capacity to astonish us with something new or different, often recognizable in your ability to highlight even the slightest detail, always carefully studied, above all in terms of their practical construction, revealing extraordinary "skill," both in the knowledge of different building materials and in their applicative capabilities.

Architecture and art
"Allegory," wrote Benjamin, "is not a playful illustrative technique, but a form of expression, just as speech is expression, and, indeed, just as writing is." The plastic character of the symbol, where the idea is instantly embodied in a form, is op-

"A relationship between space and time exists in the theater, and it is a relationship of the utmost importance—the definition of theatrical space is determined by the time of the action."

"The stage is a recognizable place, even though the theatrical space is in constant transformation. In every set, recognizable, codifiable elements are superimposed: going to and returning from somewhere, accessible-inaccessible. Staying somewhere, lasting-not lasting. Being somewhere in a certain way; recognizable-unrecognizable."

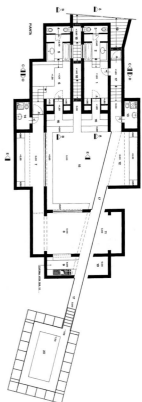

Project of a villa at Cap Ferrat, 1978
Plan

posed by the temporal character of allegory, where history is fixed in the "requisite."

Allegories are to the reign of ideas what ruins are to the reign of things, or what words are to a language: coded symbols filled with meaning. In architecture, which is allegorical form, the object has always had the capacity to define space. But today, this has changed, because the subject and its position in space have changed radically, therefore we now need to create a new triple relationship between subject-object-space, which in turn are related to time. Every building gives form to time, therefore the form of built architecture is the form of the time that produces it, because architecture is also a symbol, as well as an allegory. In fact, it is one of the constructive symbols of Western thought; it is not just a discipline, but also something that filters horizontally into all other fields.

Dear Gae, it's very difficult for me to identify the point in your work where architecture ends and art begins. As I said in the introduction, you design yourself as part of your ongoing and total designing of things and houses for man. And it's precisely inside this "total designing" that I would like to identify the fact that for you each "drift" that the project is allowed to make toward art is strictly controlled, or in other words always directed inside the complex composition system required by the architectural project. While it is true that even if your output is often provocative and the result of spontaneous intuition, which suddenly intervenes as in any artistic production, once built, it manages to present itself with a decidedly "definitive" appearance that is strongly architectural and scientific, as well as being artistic. For example, I am thinking of your work in the field of design, the stage sets and the numerous designs for installations, exhibits and temporary or permanent exhibitions. One of the temporary exhibitions that impressed me most—to the extent that I decided to make it the subject of an article in a special issue of "Anfione Zeto," a magazine that I founded and still edit—is the extraordinary "sign" that you "designed" inside Wright's Guggenheim Museum. In the first book on your work that I edited, Gino Valle said that you superimposed yourself on the master with "determined violence," not out of lack of respect but rather to induce a new perception of space and movement which was functional to the exhibition, and also the

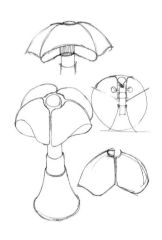

Studies for the Pipistrello lamp, 1965

need to make the existing architecture "live again" in different ages, starting afresh on each occasion.

Today the user value and the trade value of all manufactured objects are basically linked to their cost in monetary terms. The modernist and functionalist avant-garde has been overwhelmed by capital and absorbed into the cycle of production-consumption; it has lost its most authentic value and its true usefulness. Instead, according to "arte povera," it is possible to rethink the binomials of use-value and meaning-value; what is not useful may equally have a meaning, and similarly what is meaningless or useless may be important. But although this may be true of art, we are left with a problem: is there any sense in architecture that cannot be used, architecture that lacks the symbolic representativeness of using meaning? Architecture cannot be equated with waste or lack of form, precisely because it is repository of a function. Art can be "useless," but architecture cannot because it meets a need. Does art that withstands the enticing temptation of fashion and dissolving into communication, art that retains its incommunicable essence have something in common with architecture?

Our time is experiencing a constant process of "overtaking:" above all, ideologies, but also forms and criticisms; the fact of being "post," or posthumous in every sense, justifies our ability to create things that are both useful and useless, pregnant with meaning and meaningless, endowed with form and formless.

What can "saying yes" to our time mean? Can someone still exist who draws his form from an interior principle that represents to him both structure and law? Does the form that dominates him necessarily have to be similar in principle to that which moulds everything around him? I believe that it is essential, for an architect, to organize his work in the light of these questions, which as such interact with thought and "open up" the possibility of building not merely a work, but a work of art.

"By definition temporary exhibitions introduce new systems of knowledge around the protagonists, movements, and artistic schools, creating new cognitive tensions. They have a stupefying seductive power and therefore they tend to present broader working hypotheses."

Re-use of the Lingotto, international invited competition, 1983
Detail of perspective

LIST OF WORKS

*(projects marked with a triangle are
published in this volume)*

1956 San Siro, Milan
Single family house with stable
1959 Camisasca, Como
Single family villa
with Luisa Castiglioni
1959 Milan
Apartment in Via Turati
1959 Milan
House-studio in Via Cesariano
1960 Brescia
Regional competition for the Palazzo
dell'Economia
with Michele Achilli, Daniele Brigidini,
Guido Canella
1960 Modena
Regional competition for the head office of the Cassa di Risparmio
with Michele Achilli, Daniele Brigidini,
Guido Canella
1960
Central bookshelf for Tornaghi
1960
Furniture series for Anguillesi
with Sergio Rizzi and Aldo Rossi
1960 Milan
Layout and participation in the *New
Designs for Italian Furniture* exhibition
at the Osservatore delle Arti Industriali, Via San Pietro all'Orto 9
with Guido Canella
1960 Milan
XII Triennale, Apartment in the city
centre and Entrance to Triennale from
the Park
with Luigi Caccia Dominioni, Pier Fausto Bagatti Valsecchi, Elena Balsari,
Romano Beretta, Antonio Grandi
▶ **1962**
Sgarsul rocking chair
for Poltronova *(p. 211)*
1962 Monza, Milan
Provincial competition for a Primary
School
▶ **1962** Passo del Tonale, Trento
Holiday Centre
with Tekne S.p.A. *(p. 140)*

▶ **1963**
Stringa furniture series
for Poltronova *(p. 214)*
▶ **1963**
House in the wood *(p. 18)*
1963 Cesano Boscone, Milan
Residential buildings
with Tekne S.p.A.
1963 Milan
Design Centre in Via Visconti di Mo-
drone
1963 Milan
Building in Via Morigi
1963 Milan
Furnishing for the Hotel
Principe & Savoia
▶ **1964**
Giova table lamp for Poltronova / Fontana Arte *(p. 213)*
▶ **1964**
Aprilina folding chair
for Zanotta *(p. 216)*
1964 Milan
Residential buildings in Corso di Porta
Vittoria
with Tekne S.p.A.
▶ **1964** Milan
XIII Milan Triennale, Italian Section
Il tempo delle vacanze (p. 142)
▶ **1964-1965**
Locus Solus furniture series for Poltronova / Zanotta *(p. 210)*
▶ **1965**
Pipistrello table lamp
for Martinelli Luce *(p. 206)*
▶ **1965**
Jumbo marble table
for Knoll *(p. 219)*
1965 Milan
Max Mara offices and showroom
1966 Broni, Pavia
Gardens in Piazza Libertà
▶ **1967** Paris
Olivetti Showroom *(p. 144)*
▶ **1967**
King Sun table lamp
for Kartell *(p. 212)*
▶ **1967**
Ruspa table lamp
for Martinelli Luce *(p. 207)*
▶ **1967-1993**
Rimorchiatore table lamp
for Candle / Fontana Arte *(p. 213)*
▶ **1968** Buenos Aires
Olivetti Showroom *(p. 146)*
1968 Meda, Milan
Competition for a Primary School
(winning project)
with Vico Magistretti

▶ **1968**
Oracolo and *Mezzoracolo* series of
lamps for Artemide *(p. 208)*
▶ **1968**
Gae Aulenti furniture series
for Kartell *(p. 220)*
1968
Arcata furniture series
for Poltronova
1968
Eco furniture series for T70
1968 Boston
Knoll International Showroom
1968 Milan
Furnishing for Palace Hotel
1968 Milan
Cadette boutique and showroom
1968 Parly 2, Paris
Dior shop
1968 Turin
FIAT pavilion at the Motor Show
1969
Elements for the presentation of FIAT
vehicles
1969
Wrist watch for Zenith
1969 Geneva
FIAT pavilion at the Motor Show
1969 Milan
Apartment in Via Gabba
1969 Milan
Apartment in Via Borgospesso
▶ **1969** Milan
House for an Art Collector *(p. 148)*
1969 Milan
House-studio in Via Annunciata
1969 Milan
FIAT Showroom in Via Dante and Via
Fabio Filzi
1969 New York
Knoll International Showroom
1969 Paris
Pan American Clipper Club, Orly Air-
port
1969 Rome
Pan American Clipper Club, Fiumicino
Airport
1969 Turin
FIAT pavilion at the Motor Show
▶ **1969-70** Paris, Barcelona, Madrid,
Edinburgh, Tokyo
Layout of Olivetti travelling exhibition
Concept and Form (p. 150)
▶ **1970** Tuscany
Garden *(p. 20)*
1970 Turin
FIAT Showroom in Via Roma
▶ **1970** Zurich
FIAT Showroom *(p. 152)*

1970
Tamigi stainless steel cutlery
for Bacci
1970 Brussels
FIAT Showroom
1970 Geneva
FIAT pavilion at the Motor Show
1970 Mendrisio
Single family house
1970 Milan
New head office for Voxson
1970 Milan
Knoll International Showroom
1970 Turin
FIAT pavilion at the Motor Show
1970 Vienna
FIAT Showroom
1970-1975 Villa Opicina, Trieste
Redesign and project for extension of
the Hotel Obelisco
1971 Florence
Apartment with roof terrace
▶ **1971**
April folding armchair
for Zanotta
(p. 217)
▶ **1971**
Tennis furniture series
for Knoll *(p. 209)*
1971
Festo series of tables
for Zanotta
1971 Amsterdam
Offices for Thyssen-Bornemisza Group
1971 Capalbio, Grosseto
Single family villa
1971 Milan
Chairman's offices for the
Banca Commerciale Italiana
1971 Paraggi, Genoa
Single family house
1971 Paris
Single family house
1971 Perugia
International competition for the Business Center
1971 S. Margherita Ligure, Genoa
Single family house
1971 Voghera, Pavia
Bus station
1972 Amalfi, Salerno
The Grotta Rosa
1972
Kukka sofa for Zanotta
1972
Pileo, Mezzopileo, Pileino series of
lamps for Artemide
1972 Broni, Pavia
Primary School

1972 Cap d'Antibes
Remodelling of Château de la Crôe
1972 Milan
Montedison Centre in Via Cavallotti
1972 Milan
Project for "Milan instead of Milan.
Transforming the way of life by transforming the traffic."
ADI International competition
"The city as a meaningful environment "
with Nanni Cagnone, Corrado Cresciani, Antonello Maniscalco, Elsa Milani,
Roberto Pieraccini, Luigi Respighi, Richard Sapper, Sandra Severi Sarfatti,
Takashi Shimura, Maurizio Turchet
1972 Milan
Gabbianelli Stand at Eurodomus
▶ **1972** New York
Participation in *Italy: The New Domestic Landscape* exhibition at the Museum of Modern Art *(p. 224)*
1972 Rome
Apartment at Torre del Grillo
1972 Lugano
Rodin pavilion
1972-1976
Tre Più series of spotlights for Stilnovo
with Piero Castiglioni
1973 San Michele di Pagana, Genoa
Single family house
▶ **1973** Pisa
Single family house *(p. 22)*
1973
Manual for the layout of FIAT showrooms
1973
Tripolina folding armchair
for Zanotta
1973
Furniture series for Zanotta (*Ottomano* sofa, *Bettone* bed, *Gaetano* and
Briscolo tables)
1973 Cinisello Balsamo, Milan
Neighbourhood for 3500 inhabitants
with Primary School and Middle School
1973 Milan
Installation for the *Christo* exhibit at
the Rotonda della Besana
1973 Milan
Apartment in Via Fiori Oscuri
1973 Milan
Single family house in Via Pascoli
1973 Montecarlo
Mediterraneo restaurant
at the Hotel Mirabeau
1973 New York
Branch office of the Banca Commerciale Italiana

1973 Paraggi, Genoa
Single family villa "La Besozza"
1973 Rome
Pineto residential district
1973 Viareggio, Lucca
"Galleria del libro" bookshop
1974
Stage design for *Le astuzie femminili*
by Domenico Cimarosa
Director: Luca Ronconi
Teatro Mediterraneo, Naples
1974
Singa lamp for Francesconi
1974
Linea series of bathroom fittings
for Pozzi-Ginori
1974 Formentor, Balearic Islands
Single family villa
1974 Milan
Apartment in Via Gesù
1974 Milan
House-studio in Piazza San Marco
1974 Rome
Apartment in Tor de' Specchi
▶ **1974-1975**
Preliminary studies for *Utopia* by Aristophanes *(p. 82)*
▶ **1975** Parma
Single family house *(p. 154)*
▶ **1975**
Patroclo table lamp
for Artemide *(p. 204)*
1975
Alcinoo table lamp
for Artemide
1975
Stage design for *Il barbiere di Siviglia*
by Gioachino Rossini
Conductor: Diego Masson
Director: Luca Ronconi
Théâtre National Odéon, Paris
1975
Totem series of lamps for Stilnovo
1975
Lira, Cassiopea, Acquario, Orione furniture series for Elam
1975
Lettura furniture series
for Planula
1975 Broni, Pavia
Nuova Italia Gardens
1975 Galliano, Como
Garden of the Basilica
1975 Milan
Apartment in Via Bigli
1975 Cap Ferrat
Single family villa
1976
Glicine series of lamps for Vistosi

1976
Gae Aulenti collection furniture series for Knoll
1976 Milan
Exhibition design for *Cento anni, cento firme nel Corriere della Sera* at Sforza Castle with Roberto Pieraccini
1976 Milan
Apartment in Via Tessa
1976 Milan
Apartment in Via Piatti
1976 Milan
Offices in Via Cino del Duca
1976 Turin
FIAT pavilion at the Motor Show
▶ **1976-1978** Prato
Theater Planning Workshop
with Luca Ronconi *(p. 84)*
1976-1978
Preliminary studies for *La vita è sogno* by Calderón de la Barca
Theater Planning Workshop, Prato
1977
Stage design for *Wozzeck* by Alban Berg
Conductor: Claudio Abbado
Director: Luca Ronconi
Costumes: Giovanna Buzzi
Teatro alla Scala, Milan
Théâtre de l'Opéra, Paris
1977 Geneva
Layout for Bulgari exhibition at Crisart S.A.
1977 Kassel
Layout of *Christo* exhibition at the Orangerie
1977 Milan
Apartment in Via Spiga
1977 Milan
Apartment in Via Durini
1977 Zoagli, Genoa
Apartment
▶ **1977-1978**
Stage design for *The Wild Duck* by Henrik Ibsen
Director: Luca Ronconi
Costumes: Vera Marzot
1977: Teatro Metastasio, Prato. Teatro Verdi, Pisa. Teatro Duse, Genoa. Teatro Lirico, Milan. Teatro del Palazzo dei Congressi, Bologna. Teatro Comunale, Modena. Teatro Donizetti, Bergamo. Teatro Argentina, Rome
1978: Teatro Alfieri, Turin. Teatro Comunale, Ferrara. Teatro Alighieri, Ravenna *(p. 90)*
1977-1978 Caracas
Residential complex

1978
Stage design for *Calderón* by Pier Paolo Pasolini
Director: Luca Ronconi
Theater Planning Workshop Teatro Metastasio, Prato
1978
Stage design for *La torre* by Hugo von Hofmannstahl
Director: Luca Ronconi
Theater Planning Workshop Il Fabbricone, Prato
1978
Stage design for *The Bacchae* by Euripides
Director: Luca Ronconi
Theater Planning Workshop Istituto Magnolfi, Prato
1978
OTTO A series of handles
for Fusital/Valli & Valli
1978
Bût furniture series for
Di Ronco/ICAR
1978 Cannes
International competition for the new Palais des Festivals
with Kenzo Tange
1978 Gubbio, Perugia
Casa La Rosa
1978 Gubbio, Perugia
Single family house
1978 Lindos (Greece)
Single family house
1978 London
Apartment
1978 St. Moritz
Chesa Alcyon
1978 Turin
FIAT pavilion at the Motor Show
1979
Drawing board for Zucor
1979 Milan
Consultation invited of the magazine "Casabella" for Zone 2
Isola-Garibaldi-Porta Nuova
1979 Milan
Apartment in Via Borgonuovo
1979 Milan
Apartment in Via Cappuccio
1979 Paris
Cacharel shops
▶ **1979-1980**
Stage design for *Opera* by Luciano Berio
Conductor: Marcello Panni
Director: Luca Ronconi
Costumes: Giovanna Buzzi
1979: Théâtre de l'Opéra, Lyon. Maison de la Culture, Nanterre

1980: Teatro Regio, Turin. Teatro dell'Opera, Rome *(p. 92)*
1979-1987 San Rossore, Pisa
Società Alfea racecourse
▶ **1980**
Parola serie of lamps
for Fontana Arte
with Piero Castiglioni *(p. 215)*
1980
Medusa and Minibox series of lamps for Stilnovo
with Piero Castiglioni
1980
Silver tea service for Cleto Munari, production Rossi & Arcandi
▶ **1980**
Crystal table with wheels for Schopenhauer/Fontana Arte *(p. 223)*
1980 Cannes
Single family house
1980 Milan
Showroom Fontana Arte
1980 Milan
Apartment in Via Borgonuovo
▶ **1980-1986** Paris
Musée d'Orsay *(p. 26)*
1981 Milan
Apartment in Via Santa Valeria
1981
Melograno Series of sofas for Casanova
▶ **1981**
Stage design for *Donnerstag aus Licht* by Karlheinz Stockhausen
Conductor: Peter Eotvos
Director: Luca Ronconi
Costumes: Giovanna Buzzi
Teatro alla Scala, Milan *(p. 96)*
▶ **1981**
Nina table lamp for Fontana Arte *(p. 218)*
1981
Drawing table and drawing machine for Bieffe
▶ **1981-1989**
Stage design for *La donna del lago* by Gioachino Rossini
Conductor: Maurizio Pollini
Director and stage designer: Gae Aulenti
Costumes: Giovanna Buzzi
1981-1983
Rossini Opera Festival, Pesaro
1986: Teatro Comunale G.Verdi, Trieste (Conductor: Maurizio Arena.
Director: Ugo Tessitore)
Théâtre de l'Opera, Nice (Conductor: Claire Gibault. Director: Ugo Tessitore)
1989: Teatro Regio, Parma
(Conductor: Arnold Oestman.
Director: Gae Aulenti) *(p. 98)*

1982
Ginestra and *Erica* furniture series for Casanova
1982
TRE A series of handles
for Fusital/Valli & Valli
1982
Maria Politas furniture series for Trois Suisses
1982
2720 crystal table for
Schopenhauer/Fontana Arte
1982 Milan
Apartment in Piazza Castello
1982 Paris
Guest-quarters and Offices on Champs Elysées
1982-1985 Cernobbio, Como
Exhibition pavilion, Grand Hotel Villa d'Este
▶ **1982-1985** Paris
National Museum of Modern Art in Georges Pompidou Centre *(p. 34)*
1983
Stage design for *Flug in die Anden* by Michel Vinaver
Director: Arie Zinger
Costumes: Giovanna Buzzi
Residenztheater, Munich
1983 Milan
Apartment in Via dei Pellegrini
1983 Portofino, Genoa
Apartment
1983 St. Moritz
Chesa Margunz
▶ **1983** Turin
International invited competition "Twenty projects for the future of the Lingotto" *(p. 156)*
▶ **1984**
Stage design for *Samstag aus Licht* by Karlheinz Stockhausen
Conductor: Karlheinz Stockhausen
Director: Luca Ronconi
Costumes: Giovanna Buzzi
Palazzo dello Sport, Milan. Produzione Teatro alla Scala, Milan *(p. 94)*
1984
Rossini/Gae furniture series
for Cappellini/Maxalto
1984 Milan
Apartment in Via Fiori Oscuri
1984 Milan
Office for Banca Commerciale Italiana
▶ **1984-2001**
Stage design for *Il viaggio a Reims* by Gioachino Rossini
Conductor: Claudio Abbado
Director: Luca Ronconi

Costumes: Giovanna Buzzi
Auditorium Pedrotti, Rossini Opera Festival, Pesaro
1985: Teatro alla Scala, Milan
1988: Staatsoper, Vienna
1992: Teatro Comunale, Ferrara; Teatro Rossini, Rossini Opera Festival, Pesaro.
Conductor: Daniele Gatti
1999: Palafestival, Rossini Opera Festival, Pesaro
2001: Teatro Comunale, Bologna
(p. 100)
1985 Paris
Cerruti 1881 shop
1985 Milan
Apartment J.V.
1985 Milan
Participation in XVII Milan Triennale *Elective Affinities* with the project *The harmonious box. The room of mirrors.* with Mariani and Colnaghi, Lissone
1985 Milan
Participation in exhibition *Ten proposals for Milan*, Milan Triennale, with the project for Piazza Formentini
1985 New York
Marina B shop
1985
Stage design for *Rigoletto* by Giuseppe Verdi, *La fanciulla del West* by Giacomo Puccini, *Cavalleria Rusticana* by Pietro Mascagni, *Pagliacci* by Ruggero Leoncavallo
Director: Virginia Westlake
Pasquale D'Ascola, Mattia Testi
Costumes: Giovanna Buzzi
IX Estate Musicale, Rocca Brancaleone, Ravenna
▶ **1985-1986** Venice
Remodelling of Palazzo Grassi *(p. 158)*
▶ **1985-2004** Barcelona
National Museum of Catalan Art in Palau Nacional de Montjuic *(p. 38)*
1986
Interior Design for a sailing boat
with Giorgetti & Magrini, Milan
1986 Rome
Pirelli head offices
1986
Bugia and *Diamante* lamps
for Fontana Arte
with Piero Castiglioni
▶ **1986** Milan
International invited competition for the transformation of the Pirelli area of the Bicocca *(p. 157)*
1986 Milan
Techint new head office

▶ **1986** Venice
Layout for the exhibition *Futurism & Futurisms* at Palazzo Grassi *(p. 158)*
1986-1989 Milan
Guest quarters of the Banca Commerciale Italiana
1986-1991 Venice
New Theatre at Palazzo Grassi
1986-1994
Cestello lighting system for Guzzini with Piero Castiglioni
1987
Minuetto sofa for Poltrona Frau
1987
Marble bench for
Ultima Edizione
1987
Lapsus crystal coffee table for Fontana Arte
1987 Barcelona
Installation for the First Cinema Festival with Beth Galì
1987 Cremona
Layout of exhibition *Antonio Stradivari 1737-1987* at Palazzo Comunale
1987 Rome
New campus for the Libera Università Internazionale di Studi Sociali (L.U.I.S.S.)
1987 St. Moritz
Chesa Mezdi-Jadoroco
1987 Venice
Installation for the Heads of State Summit meeting at Palazzo Grassi
1987-1991 Tolentino, Macerata
Single family house
1987-1992 Dallas, Houston,
Los Angeles, Palm Beach, San Francisco, St. Louis, Toronto, Buenos Aires, Tokyo "Adrienne Vittadini" stores
1987-1992 Berlin
International invited competition for the restoration of the former Italian Embassy for the Academy of Science
1987-2000 Prato
Civic Museum in Palazzo Pretorio
with Bianca Ballestrero
▶ **1987-2000** Biella
"Città degli Studi" and detached campus of the Turin Polytechnic *(p. 46)*
▶ **1988**
Pietra table lamp for Fontana Arte
with Piero Castiglioni *(p. 219)*
1988
Wrist watch, ballpoint pen, fountain pen and pencil
for Louis Vuitton
1988
Tonda series of bathroom fittings and *Iperbole* taps for Ideal Standard

▶**1988**
Stage design for *Zar Saltan* by Nikolaj Rimskij-Korsakov
Conductor: Vladimir Fedosseev
Director: Luca Ronconi
Costumes: Giovanna Buzzi
Teatro Municipale Romolo Valli, Reggio Emilia. Teatro Lirico, Milan (produzione Teatro alla Scala, Milan)
(p. 102)
1988 Gavi, Alessandria
Single family house
1988 Milan
Attic flat in Via Cino del Duca
1988 Milan
S.B.S. Offices
1988 Venice
Layout of exhibition *The Phoenicians* at Palazzo Grassi
1988-1991 Geneva
Apartment
1988-1991 Rome
Remodelling of the Palazzo Muti-Bussi
1988-1992 Sassuolo, Modena
Remodelling of the Palazzina della Casiglia
1988-1994 Bologna
Remodelling of Head office for Credito Emiliano
1988-1994 Osmate, Varese
Single family villa
1989 Milan
Layout of exhibition *Teatro alla Scala 1789-1989* at the Teatro alla Scala Museum
1989 Milan
Marina B shop
1989 Turin
Exhibition layout for *Altra Ego. The photograph seen by Josif Brodskij. Faces dear to the soul for the poets from Baudelaire to Pasolini* at the Mole Antonelliana
1989 Venice
Layout of exhibition *Italian Art. Presences 1900-1945* at Palazzo Grassi
1989-1991 Naples
Remodelling of Istituto Universitario "Suor Orsola Benincasa"
1989-1993 Fermo, Ascoli Piceno
Remodelling of Teatro dell'Aquila
1990
Suor Orsola standing lamp for Fontana Arte
with Piero Castiglioni
1990
Stage design for *Ricciardo e Zoraide* by Gioachino Rossini

Conductor: Riccardo Chailly
Director: Luca Ronconi
Costumes: Giovanna Buzzi
Rossini Opera Festival, Pesaro
1990 Paris
Layout of *Euphronios* exhibition at the Louvre Museum
1990 Paris
Marina B shop
1990 Tremezzo, Como
Single family house
1990 Venice
Layout for the exhibition *Andy Warhol. A retrospective* at Palazzo Grassi
1990 Venice
Layout for the exhibition *From Van Gogh to Picasso, from Kandinskij to Pollock* at Palazzo Grassi
1990 Vienna
Layout for the exhibition *Zaubertöne. Mozart in Wien* at the Künstlerhaus
▶ **1990** Florence
Entrance to S. Maria Novella Station with Bianca Ballestrero *(p. 50)*
▶ **1990** St. Tropez
Single family villa *(p. 48)*
1990 Turin
Pavilion with swimming pool
1990 Milan
Offices for Partners Srl
1991 Milan
Apartment in Via Cino del Duca
1991 Milan
Offices for Finsimi SpA
1991 Rome
Apartment in Via Pinciana
1991
Eva standing lamp in kevlar for Stilnovo
1991
Tlinkit armchair in rattan for TECNO
1991 Berlin
Layout for the exhibition *Euphronios* at the Dahlem Museum
1991 Berlin
International invited competition for the "Zentraler Omnibus Bahnof" area
▶ **1991** Paris
International invited competition for the redesign of the "Salle des Etats" at the Louvre Museum *(p. 160)*
1991 Venice
Layout for the exhibition *The Celts* at Palazzo Grassi
1991-1993 Milan
Acoustic shell for the Teatro alla Scala
1991-1993 Milan
Apartment in Via Fiori Oscuri

1991-1994 Milan
Remodelling of Palazzina del Fornaio
1991-1996 Torrecchia Vecchia, Latina
Single family house
1991-1996 Città di San Marino, RSM
Remodelling of the Palazzo del Governo
1991-1996 Milan
Tower office building in the technology district Pirelli-Bicocca
▶**1992** Seville
Italian pavilion at EXPO '92
with Pierluigi Spadolini *(p. 54)*
1992
Totem, wooden container on wheels for TECNO
1992
Aldabra series of lamps for Fontana Arte
with Piero Castiglioni
1992
Kum office furniture series for TECNO
1992 Florence
Layout for the exhibition *The White Room: the birth of Italian Fashion* at Palazzo Strozzi
▶ **1992** Milan
Set for the television programme *Una storia* presented by Enzo Biagi on RAI 1 *(p. 104)*
1992 Rome
Apartment in Via Due Macelli
1992 Tokyo
International invited competition for the Sakuraokacho Hotel-Office Building with Ishimoto Architecture & Engineering Inc. and RTKL Ltd.
1992 Washington D.C.
Invited competition for the New Chaucery of the Italian Embassy
1992 Istanbul
Greater Istanbul Municipality Nejat F. Eczacibasi Art Museum
with Resit Soley
1992 Rome
Museum of Energy ENEL SpA
1992-1995 Gallarate, Varese
Single family villa
1992-1996
Interior design for a sailing boat with German Frers
1993 Milan
Banner shop
1993
Etra kitchen for Snaidero/ABACO
1993
Mediterraneo series of shop furnishings for ISA SpA

1993
Tour crystal table with bicycle wheels for Schopenhauer/Fontana Arte
(p. 222)
1993 Paris
Layout for the exhibition *La Renaissance de la Mode Italienne* at the Musée des Arts de la Mode et du Textile, Louvre
1993 Saragoza
International invited competition for the Aragon Museum of Contemporary Art
1993 Venice
Layout for the exhibition *Marcel Duchamp* at Palazzo Grassi
1993 Venice
Layout for the exhibition *Modigliani, from the collection of Dottor Paul Alexandre* at Palazzo Grassi
1993 Venice
Retail space at Palazzo Grassi
1993-1995 Milan
Feasibility study for the Sforza Castle
1993-1996 Milan
Façade of a building in Largo Richini
▶ **1994**
Stage design for *Elektra* by Richard Strauss
Conductor: Giuseppe Sinopoli
Director: Luca Ronconi
Costumes: Giovanna Buzzi
Teatro alla Scala, Milan *(p. 108)*
▶ **1994**
Stage design for *Il mondo della luna* by Franz Joseph Haydn
Conductor: Salvatore Accardo
Director: Costa-Gavras
Costumes: Giovanna Buzzi
Teatro San Carlo, Naples *(p. 106)*
1994
Tableware
for Argenterie Greggio
1994
Tisa silver pot for herbal tea
for Faraone
1994 Milan
Mandarina Duck shop
1994 Biella
Updating of General Town-planning Scheme
with Gaetano Lisciandra
▶ **1994** Milan
Temporary Exhibition Gallery at Milan Triennale *(p. 166)*
▶ **1994** New York
Layout for the exhibition *The Italian Metamorphosis, 1943-1968* at the Solomon R. Guggenheim Museum *(p. 162)*

1994 Valencia
Layout for the exhibition *Fausto Melotti* at the Institut Valencià d'Art Modern (IVAM)
1995 London
Redesign and extension of a single family house
▶ **1995**
Torto, Ritorto, Sfera, Geacolor blown glass vases for Venini *(p. 205)*
1995
Perdue small beech armchair for Schopenhauer/Fontana Arte
▶ **1995**
Stage design for *King Lear* by William Shakespeare
Director: Luca Ronconi
Costumes: Rudy Sabounghi
Teatro Argentina, Rome
Teatro Lirico, Milan *(p. 8)*
1995
Aralia furniture series for Schopenhauer/Fontana Arte
1995 Venice
Layout for the Centenary of the Biennale exhibition *Identity and Otherness. A short history of the human body 1895-1995* at Palazzo Grassi and in the Italian Pavilion in the Gardens
1995 Venice
Layout for the exhibition *Open Palace. Scenes of Venetian life by Gabriel Bella and Pietro Longhi, from the Querini Stampalia Foundation* at Palazzo Grassi
1995 Wolfsburg
Layout for the exhibition *Die italenische Metamorphose 1943-1968* at the Kunstmuseum
1995 Ibiza
Single family house
1995-in progress Udine
Remodelling of Casa Colombatti-Cavazzini and Lascito Ferrucci. Museum of the Astaldi Collection
1995 Paris
G.A. Apartment
1996 Milan
Tivioli Showroom
1996 Monza, Milan
Residential and commercial development
1996
Toast toaster for Trabo
1996 Venice
Layout for the exhibition *The Western Greeks* at Palazzo Grassi
1996 Ferrara
Feasibility study for an integrated Museum Centre for Modern and Contemporary Art with Gaetano Lisciandra

1996 Ferrara
Layout for the exhibition *Pompei. Living under Vesuvius* at Palazzo dei Diamanti
▶ **1996** Florence
Piazza in front of the former "Leopolda" station
with Bianca Ballestrero *(p. 168)*
▶ **1996** Melbourne
International competition for the renovation of the National Gallery of Victoria with Denton Corker Marshall, Melbourne *(p. 116)*
▶ **1996** Oxford
International invited competition for the Business School *(p. 110)*
1996 Florence
Layout for the exhibition *The Time and Fashion*, "Visitors" section at the Florence Biennale
1996 Mairano di Casteggio, Pavia
Remodelling of Casa Rajna, Bussolera Foundation
▶ **1996-in progress** Alcamo, Trapani
Piazza Ciullo and Piazza del Mercato
(p. 114)
▶ **1996-2003** San Francisco
New Asian Art Museum
in association with the joint venture HOK/LDA/RWA *(p. 58)*
▶ **1997** Venice
International tender-competition for the reconstruction of La Fenice Theatre with temporary Grouping of Companies: Impregilo SpA, Fiatengineering, ICCEM Srl, COVECO, SACAIM SpA (p. 118)
▶ **1997** Shanghai
Linhu Villas
with Impregilo SpA, Shanghai *(p.124)*
1997 Milan
Apartment in Corso Garibaldi
1997
Series of doors for COCIF
1997 Venice
Layout for the exhibition *Flemish and Dutch Painting. From Van Gogh, Ensor, Magritte, Mondrian to the Contemporaries* at Palazzo Grassi
1997 Venice
Layout for the exhibition in the Corderie dell'Arsenale and Gardens. 47th International Art Exhibition, Venice Biennale
1997 Venice
Layout for the exhibition *German Expressionism: Art and Society* at Palazzo Grassi
▶ **1997** Milan
Palazzo della Ragione *(p. 172)*

1997 Rome
Salone dei Corazzieri at the Palazzo del Quirinale
1997 Rimini
New headquarters for Provincial government
▶ **1997** San Casciano in Val di Pesa, Florence
New Town Hall (p. 122)
1997-2001 Venice, Milan, Genoa, Montecarlo, Brussels, San Paolo, Paris, Tokyo
Layout for the exhibition Pirelli Calendars 1964-1997/2001
1998 Venice
Layout for the exhibition Picasso 1917-1924 at Palazzo Grassi
1998 Andria, Bari
Public services building in Castel del Monte
1998 Paris
Apartment in rue Fabert
1998 Lerici, La Spezia
Funerary monument
1998 Maratea, Potenza
General Town-planning Scheme
with Gaetano Lisciandra
▶ **1998** Florence
International consultation invited for the new exit from the Uffizi in Piazza Castellani
with Bianca Ballestrero (p. 126)
1998-in progress Tokyo
International competition for the Italian Institute of Culture and redesign of the Chaucery of the Italian Embassy (winning project)
with Kajima Corp.
▶ **1998-in progress** Jerusalem
Extension for a Hotel (p. 62)
1998-in progress Venaria, Turin
Restoration and requalification of the Royal Palace
1999
Blender for TRABO
▶ **1999** Milan
Spazio Oberdan
with Carlo Lamperti-Archicat (p.174)
▶ **1999** Rome
Renovation and functional adapation of former Papal Stables at the Quirinale and layout for the exhibition One Hundred Impressionists Masterpieces from the Hermitage and Historical Avantgardes (p. 178)
1999 Rome
Preliminary project for the new layout of the "piano nobile" of Palazzo del Quirinale

1999 Venice
Layout for the exhibition The Renaissance in Venice and painting in the North in the age of Bellini, Dürer, Tiziano at Palazzo Grassi
1999
Ceremonial Sword for the Académie des Beaux-Arts, Paris
1999 Rome
Entrance Foyer at Teatro Brancaccio
1999
Set for television programme Ultimo Walzer presented by Fabio Fazio on RAI 2
1999 Athens
New Concert Hall
with Carlo Lamperti-Archicat
▶ **1999** Genoa Bolzaneto
European competition for the preliminary project for a wholesale fruit, vegetable and flower market
with Metropolitana Milanese SpA (p. 182)
▶ **1999** Chiasso
International competition for the noise prevention in the Bissone-Melide zone, A2 Chiasso-San Gottardo Highway
with Marco Marcionelli, Ernst Winkler+Partner AG (p. 184)
1999 Milan
Layout for the exhibition Varon, Magg, Balestrer, Tanz, Parin. Literature in Milanese dialect from Maggi to Porta at the Biblioteca Nazionale Braidense
1999-2000 Venice, Paris, New York
Layout for the exhibition Anni Albers Retrospective, Peggy Guggenheim Collection, Venice; Pavillon de Marsan-Louvre, Paris; Jewish Museum, New York
▶ **1999-2002** Naples
"Museo" and "Dante" Stations on Underground Line 1 and redesign of Piazza Cavour and Piazza Dante (p. 66)
▶ **1999-in progress** Genoa
Functional adaptation and redefinition of exhibition layout for Edoardo Chiossone Civic Museum of Oriental Art
with Carlo Lamperti-Archicat (p. 64)
▶ **2000** Milan
Piazzale Cadorna and the new façade of the Ferrovie Nord (p. 186)
2000 Positano, Salerno
Fitness Centre, Hotel Le Sirenuse
2000 Biumo, Varese
Remodelling of the former Stables and design of reception area at Villa Menafoglio Litta Panza - FAI, Fondo

per l'Ambiente Italiano (Italian Heritage Trust)
2000 Venice
Layout for the exhibition Cosmos, from Goya to De Chirico, from Friedrich to Kiefer. Art in search of the infinite at Palazzo Grassi
2000 Castellazzo di Bollate, Milan
Restoration of Villa Arconati and residential development in the borgo
2000 Mozzate, Como
New complex of Primary Schools
2000 Biumo, Varese
Layout for the exhibition Giovanni Segantini. Light and symbol 1884-1899 at Villa Menafoglio Litta Panza
2000 Verona
International competition to design the new cultural center "Arsenale 2000: City of nature and music"
▶ **2000** New York
International competition for The Museum of Women, Leadership Center with HOK, New York (p. 130)
▶ **2000-in progress** Taranto
Hotel and tourist development in the province of Taranto (p. 70)
2000-in progress Cremona
New management headquarters for the Banca di Credito Cooperativo del Cremonese
▶ **2001** Plan-les-Ouates, Geneva
International invited competition for new factory with offices (p. 134)
▶ **2001** Milan
Layout for the exhibition 1951-2001 Made in Italy?, section "Memory", at Milan Triennale (p. 190)
2001 Biumo, Varese
Layout for the exhibition Art of the bicycle from Duchamp to Rauschenberg at Villa Menafoglio Litta Panza
▶ **2001** Venice
Layout for the exhibition Balthus at Palazzo Grassi (p. 159)
▶ **2001-in progress** Rimini
New office headquarters (p. 72)
2001-in progress Rome
Remodelling of the former cinema in Palazzo Altieri
▶ **2001-in progress** Piedmont
Nursery School (p. 74)
▶ **2001-in progress** Bari
Remodelling of Villa Capriati as a Contemporary Arts and Design Gallery (p. 76)
▶ **2001-in progress** Meina, Novara
New lakeside promenade
with Gaetano Lisciandra (p. 78)

2002 Venice
Layout for the exhibition *Towards Modern Art, from Puvis de Chavannes to Matisse and Picasso* at Palazzo Grassi
2002 Milan
Extension of the Biffi showroom
▶ **2002** Florence
International invited competition for the Museo dell'Opera del Duomo *(p. 194)*

BIOGRAPHY

1953 Graduated from the Faculty of Architecture at Milan Polytechnic
1955-1961 Member of the Movimento Studi per l'Architettura (Architectural Studies Movement)
1955-1965 Joined editorial staff of *Casabella-Continuità* under the editorship of Ernesto Nathan Rogers
1960 Member of the ADI, Associazione Disegno Industriale (Industrial Design Association)
1960-1962 Assistant to Professor Giuseppe Samonà in the Department of Architectural Composition at the University of Venice (IUAV)
1964-1969 Assistant to Professor Ernesto Nathan Rogers in the Department of Elements of Architectural Composition at the Faculty of Architecture, Milan Polytechnic
1966 Art Director of "Centro Fly Casa," Milan
1966 On the editorial staff of *La Fiera Letteraria*, a weekly review of Letters, Arts and Science, edited by Diego Fabbri
1966-1969 Vice President of the Industrial Design Association
1967 Honorary member of the American Society of Interior Designers (ASID)
1974-1979 Member of the Board of Directors of *Lotus International*
1977-1980 Member of the Executive Committee, Triennale, Milan
1984 "Accademico Corrispondente" for the Accademia Nazionale di San Luca, Rome; "Accademico" in the class of National Architects (1987); "Accademico Nazionale" (1988)
1990 Honorary Fellow of the American Institute of Architects (hon. FAIA)
1990 Honorary member of the Bund Deutscher Architekten (BDA)
1995-1996 President of the Accademia di Belle Arti di Brera, Milan

Personal exhibitions / Participation in exhibitions

1950 Invited to IX Triennale, Milan as a member of the ALSA, Associazione Libera Studenti Architetti (Free Student Architects' Association). Subject: "The Training of an Architect"
1960 Invited to the exhibition *New Italian Furniture Designs* at the Osservatore delle Arti Industriali, Milan
1963 Invited to the exhibition *Aspects of Contempoary Art*, L'Aquila
1967 Invited to the industrial design exhibition *Mediterranean Mood*, Gimbels Department Store, New York
1968 Invited to the exhibition *Design: Italian Design*, Hallmark Gallery, New York
1979 Personal exhibition at the PAC, Padiglione di Arte Contemporanea (Pavilion of Contemporary Art), Milan
1989-1993 Invited to the *GA International* exhibition, Tokyo and Osaka
1991 Invited to the Fifth International exhibition of Architecture, Venice Biennale
1991-1995 Invited to the travelling exhibition *Le Scale dello Spazio* organised by the Ministry for Foreign Affairs and the Italian Academy of Arts in London, Mexico City, Caracas, Lisbon, Barcelona, Cairo, Beirut, Istanbul, Athens, Nicosia, Tunis, New Delhi, Sydney, Melbourne
1992 *The Photography Seen by Gae Aulenti: The Second Paradise*, Mole Antonelliana, Turin

Lectures / Jury membership

1967 Invited to the 4th National ASID Conference, "Interior Design and Education in Italy," Venice
1969-1975 Lectures on Italian architecture at "Colegio de Arquitectos," Barcelona
1973 Invited to the National Convention on full-day school, Cinisello Balsamo (Milan)
1973 Invited to the International Design Conference, Aspen (Colorado)
1975 Lecture on Italian architecture at the Italian Institute of Culture, Stockholm
1976 Invited to the Convention of American Society of Interior Designers (ASID), Atlanta (Georgia)

1976 Invited to the International Congress of Women Architects, Ramsar (Iran)

1980 Invited to the "I° Simposio Internacional de Diseño Interior," Medellin (Colombia)

1984 Member of the jury for the "Musée d'Art Contemporain" competition, Montreal (Canada)

1986 Lecture at the Medical Science University, Toronto (Canada)

1986 Lecture at Columbia University, New York

1987 Member of the jury for the "Distinguished Architecture Awards," American Institute of Architects (AIA), New York Chapter

1987 Lecture at the Italian Institute of Culture, Stockholm

1987 Lecture at the Institut für Bauökonomie, University of Stuttgart

1988 Lecture at the San Francisco Museum of Modern Art and at the University of California, Berkeley

1988 Speech "Orsay: An episode or a turning point in museography?", Roberto Longhi Foundation, former Convent of Santa Verdiana, Florence

1989 Invited to the Seminar "Barcelona i l'obra de tres arquitectos contemporanis," Barcelona (with Richard Meier and Arata Isozaki)

1990 Lecture at the Faculty of Architecture, University of Oslo

1990 Lecture on Museums and Exhibitions at Villa Pignatelli, Naples

1990 Invited to the International Seminar for Studies on Ernesto Nathan Rogers, Piccolo Teatro, Milan

1990 Invited to IN/ARCH Convention "Opera Prima" (House with stable, San Siro), Triennale, Milan

1991 Attended the "Italian Architecture in Europe" symposium as part of *The Scale of Space* exhibition organised by the Ministry of Foreign Affairs and the Italian Academy of Arts and Applied Arts in London

1991 Member of the jury for selection of the "Friedrichstadt-Passagen" designs, Berlin

1991 Lecture on Museums and Exhibitions at the Refresher Course in Communication for Cultural Heritage at the Milan Polytechnic

1991 Lecture on Museums and Exhibitions at the Italian Institute of Culture, Istanbul

1991 Lecture "The Museum issue" at the invitation of Italia Nostra, Sala congressi della Provincia, Milan

1992 Lecture on the National Museum of Catalan Art in Barcelona, Auditorium of the Louvre, Paris

1992 Lecture at the "Giornate Catalane" Convention organized by the University of Bologna, Barcelona

1992 Lecture on Museums at the Scuola Normale Superiore in Pisa

1992 Invited to Conference on "Architecture and Italian Design" organized by the Foreign Press Association, Palazzo dei Giureconsulti, Milan

1992 Lecture on Design at the Royal Palace Foundation, Amsterdam

1992 Lecture at the Graduate School of Design, Harvard University, Cambridge (USA)

1993 Lecture at the Tamayo Museum (FENAM) and at the Architects' College, Mexico City

1993 Lecture on "Museums in existing buildings" at 6th National Convention of Italian Heritage Trust (FAI), Perugia

1993 Lecture at "Ambiente, Città, Museo" Restauro '93 Convention, Ferrara

1993 Lecture on "Museum, Art, Architecture" at Accademia di Belle Arti di Brera, Milan

1993 Lecture at the 5th Architecture Biennale, Buenos Aires

1993 Lectures at the Museum of Contemporary Art, at the Italian Institute of Culture and at the Olympic Planning Workshop, Sydney

1993 Lecture on "European Museum Design" at the invitation of Ho-Am Art Museum, Seoul

1994 Lecture on the Musée d'Orsay in Paris, at the Training Course at "Ordine degli Architetti" of the Province of Milan

1994 Invited by Italia Nostra to lecture on "Upgrading Sforza Castle," Sala congressi della Provincia, Milan

1994 Lecture on "Working with Music" at the "Musica Spazio Architettura" Convention at the Triennale, Milan

1994 Lecture "Musée, Expositions, Muséographie," Auditorium of the Louvre, Paris

1994 Lecture on Temporary Exhibitions at the Triennale, Milan

1995 Member of the jury for the international competition for the New National Museum of Korea, Seoul

1995 Lecture on Temporary Exhibitions at the Pacific Design Center, Los Angeles

1995 Member of the jury for "International AUDI Design Award," Ingolstadt (Germany)

1996 Lecture on "Museums and Temporary Exhibitions," Faculty of Architecture, University of Ferrara

1996 Lecture on the National Museum of Catalan Art in Barcelona, Auditorium of the Louvre, Paris

1996 Lecture on Palazzo Grassi for "Architectour '96," Church of San Samuele, Venice

1996 Seminar "The house and furniture as living spaces: Italian proposals and solutions" at the invitation of the National Institute for Foreign Trade, Shanghai

1997 Lecture "Archeological exhibitions: a comparison of requirements," Cini Foundation, Venice

1998 Invited to International Conference "French Culture nearing 2000," Monumental Complex of San Michele a Ripa, Sala dello Stenditoio, Rome

1998 Speech at the meeting/debate "The City of 2000" at the Aspen Institute Italia, Villa d'Este, Cernobbio

1998-1999 Member of the jury for the international competition "Mediterranean squares for women and for peace" organized by UNESCO and by the Gouvernorat d'Alger (Algeri)

1999 Speech at the conference on "Musées de Gênes (Civico Museo d'Arte Orientale Edoardo Chiossone)" at the Auditorium of the Louvre, Paris

1999 Lecture on the Royal Palace of Venaria at the meeting "Promotion of architectural and urban culture" organised by the Ministry for Cultural Heritage and Activities at the Monumental Complex of San Michele a Ripa, Rome

1999 Lecture "Architecture and Art" at Leonardo da Vinci Italian State Scientific Lycée, Paris

1999 Lecture on Chiossone Museum in Genoa to "Associazione Amici dell'Arte e dei Musei," Circolo Artistico Tunnel, Genoa

1999 Speech at "Giardini in Fiera," Villa Le Corti-Principe Corsini, San Casciano Val di Pesa

2000 Lecture "A new face for Milan? Citizens and town-planning and monumental remodelling" at the Cultural Centre in via Zebedia, Milan

2000 Lecture "Reinventing the Art Museum in the 21st century" at the Japan Society, New York
2000 Attended University Guidance Course organised by the Scuola Normale Superiore in Pisa
2000 Member of the jury "2000 Design Awards," AIA, New York Chapter
2000 Lecture at Third International Conference on Architecture "Art du lieu et globalization" organized by Akzo Nobel Coatings S.A. in Casablanca
2000-2001 Member of the jury for the international architectural competition "Mediterranean squares for women and for peace" organised by UNESCO and by the Municipality of Alcalà de Henares (Madrid)
2001 Lecture "Museum Architecture: towards a new network of relations" at the announcement of the winners of the Praemium Imperiale 2001, Palazzo Altemps, Rome
2001 Lecture at Asian Art Museum Annual Meeting and Closing Ceremony, San Francisco
2002 Lecture at Convention "A city and its future: The development of Perugia and university cities" organised by the Associazione Culturale per l'Università e per l'Umbria, Palazzo dei Priori, Perugia
2002 Speech "The Museum today: Development trends between global, national and local" given for the Training Course for Diplomats, Istituto Diplomatico Italiano, Rome
2002 Lecture "New Directions in Museum Design" at the Art Institute of Chicago

Awards and Recognitions

1964 International Grand Prix for the installation of the Italian Section *Il tempo delle vacanze* at the 13th Triennale, Milan
1979 The 1978 UBU Award for the best Italian stage design (*The Bacchae* by Euripides, *Calderón* by Pier Paolo Pasolini, *Der Turm* by Hugo von Hofmannstahl)
1983 "Medaille d'Architecture" from the Academie d'Architecture, Paris
1984 The 1983 Joseph Hoffmann Prize from the Hochschule für angewandte Kunst, Vienna
1987 Title of "Chevalier de la Legion d'Honneur" conferred by the President of the Republic of France, François Mitterand
1987 Title of "Commandeur dans l'Ordre des Arts et Lettres" conferred by the French Minister of Culture, Jack Lang
1987 Recognition by the "XVI Congreso de la Union Internacional de Arquitecto (UIA)" for the transformation of the Gare d'Orsay into a Museum
1988 "Dean of Architecture Award" from the Merchandise Mart of Chicago
1989 Special Award for Culture assigned by the President of the Council of Ministers of the Italian Republic
1989 "Ambrogino d'oro" award from the City of Milan
1990 "Fashion Group Award" for Architecture, New York
1991 "Praemium Imperiale" for Architecture from the Japan Art Association, Tokyo
1994 Meritorious "Culture and Art" diploma conferred by the Minister for Cultural Heritage, Alberto Ronchey
1995 Title of "Cavaliere di Gran Croce" conferred by the President of the Republic of Italy, Oscar Luigi Scalfaro
2001 Honorary degree in Fine Arts awarded by the Rhode Island School of Design, Providence R.I. (USA)

BIBLIOGRAPHY

Francesco Tentori, *Progetti e Problemi*, in "Casabella," no. 276, 1963.
Dottore Architetto Gae Aulenti, in "Quadernos de Arquitectura," no. 74, 1969.
Alberto Arbasino, *Gae Aulenti. New Force in Italian Design*, in "Vogue" (USA), July 1970.
Italo Lupi, Umberto Riva, *Il design degli architetti*, in "Zodiac," no. 20, 1970.
Italian Lessons in Living, in "Vogue" (USA), May 1972.
"SD Space Design," no. 8, 1972 (Special issue on Gae Aulenti).
"Japan Interior Design," no. 160, 1972 (Special issue on Gae Aulenti).
Gae Aulenti Designer, in "Formaluce," no. 27, 1972.
Dacia Maraini, *E tu chi eri*, Bompiani, Milan 1973.
Gabriella Drudi, *The Design of Gae Aulenti*, in "Craft Horizons," February 1976.
Karin von Behr, *Die italienische Architektin Gae Aulenti*, in "Architektur & Wohnen," no. 2, 1977.
Pier Carlo Santini, *Gae Aulenti: Architettura, Scene, Design*, in "Ottagono," no. 47, 1977.
Rita Reif, *Home and Office; Bridging the Gap*, in "The New York Times Magazine," 1977/2/13.
"L'Architecture d'Aujourd'hui," no. 189, 1977 (International Congress of Women Architects, Ramsar, Iran, 1976).
Jean-Paul Morel, *Rencontre avec Gae Aulenti*, in "Maison Francaise," no. 330, 1979.
Franco Raggi, *Da grande voglio fare una città*, in "Modo," no. 21, 1979.
Lorenzo Berni, *Architetture di Gae Aulenti, Padiglione d'Arte Contemporanea, Milano, dicembre 1979*, in "Panorama," 1979/12/17.
Gae Aulenti, Electa, Milan 1979 (catalogue of a personal exhibition at PAC, Milan, December 1979).
Maddalena Sisto, *Incontri e pretesti. La Gae*, in "Casa Vogue," no. 102, 1980.

Gae Aulenti, *Renaissance Woman*, in "Vogue" (USA), May 1985.
Vittorio Gregotti, *Building a Passage*, in "Artforum International," no. 4, 1986.
AA.VV., *Les visages multiples de Gae Aulenti*, in "Connaissance des Arts," no. 411, 1986.
Gae Aulenti e il Museo d'Orsay, "Quaderni di Casabella," supplement to "Casabella," no. 535, 1987.
Claudine Durand, *Gae Aulenti, Une femme dans l'espace*, in "Expression," no. 2, 1987.
"A+U. Architecture and Urbanism," no. 6, 1987 (Special issue on Gae Aulenti).
Carol Vogel, *The Aulenti Uproar*, in "The New York Times Magazine," 1987/11/22.
Joseph Rykwert, *Gae Aulenti's Milan. Design Passages for the Celebrated Architect*, in "AD Architectural Digest," January 1990.
Marina Gregotti, *Gae Aulenti. L'architettura è donna*, in "Elle Decor," no. 12, 1990.
AA.VV., *Quinta Mostra Internazionale di Architettura*, La Biennale, Venice / Electa, Milan 1991.
Marina Rovera, *Conversazione Gae Aulenti-Luca Ronconi*, in "Do Maggiore," April 1991.
Matilde Oriola, *Gae Aulenti*, in "Diseño Interior," no. 2, 1991.
Sandra Edwards, *Aulenti on Aulenti*, in "Elle Decor" (USA), no.17, 1991.
Franco Raggi, *Architettura e luce mediata. Colloquio con Gae Aulenti*, in "Flare," no. 5, 1991.
Gae Aulenti. Museum Architecture, introduction by Joseph Rykwert, Edizioni Tecno, Varedo 1993.
Gae Aulenti, *Musei e Mostre Temporanee*, in "Anfione Zeto," no. 11, 1995.
Michèle Leloup, *Gae Aulenti, diva d'Orsay*, in "L'Express," 1996/8/15.
Margherita Petranzan (ed.), *Gae Aulenti*, Rizzoli, Milan 1996 - Rizzoli International Publ. Inc., New York 1997.
Doris Lockhart Saatchi, *Diva Italia*, in "Blueprint," June 1998.
Carlo Fabrizio Carli, *Non solo musei*, in "AD Architectural Digest", no. 222 (Millenium), 1999.
Art of Our Time. Ten Years of the Praemium Imperiale, The Japan Art Association, International Design UK Ltd., London 1999.
Herbert Muschamp, *Designing for a world that's already filled*, in "The New York Times," 1999/5/30.
Donata Righetti, *Aulenti. Ma com'è bella la città*, in "Corriere della Sera," 1999/7/17.
Matteo Lo Presti, *Intervista a Gae Aulenti. La città ideale*, in "Ulisse 2000," no. 189, 1999.
Delfina Rattazzi, *Aulenti: Così mi metto in gioco*, in "La Repubblica," 2000/11/13.
Rinaldo Gianola, *Intervista a Gae Aulenti*, in "l'Unità," 2002/1/12.

Gae Aulenti, *Louis Kahn. Ordine nell'architettura. Un cavallo dipinto a strisce non è una zebra*, in "La Fiera Letteraria," no. 1, 1966.
Gae Aulenti, *A Milano, un grande magazzino per l'arredamento moderno*, in "Domus," no. 438, 1966.
Gae Aulenti, *Design as Postulation*, in *Italy: The New Domestic Landscape* Museum of Modern Art, New York / Centro Di, Florence 1972.
Gae Aulenti, *Appunti su Aspen*, in "Domus," no. 527, 1973.
Gae Aulenti, *L'opzione formale*, in "Design Habitat," no. 1, 1973.
Gae Aulenti, *Studio per nuove tipologie nell'edilizia scolastica in strutture urbane consolidate*, in AA.VV., *Una nuova scuola di base. Esperienze di tempo pieno*, Emme Edizioni, Milan 1973.
Gae Aulenti, *Teatro e territorio. Il Laboratorio di Prato*, in "Lotus International," no. 17, 1977.
Gae Aulenti, *Architettura e forma grafica*, in "Casabella," no. 440/441, 1978
Gae Aulenti, *Marburg*, in "Lotus International," no. 18, 1978.
Gae Aulenti, *Appunti sulla messa in scena*, in AA.VV., *Al gran sole carico d'amore. Per un nuovo teatro musicale*, Ricordi, Milan 1978.
Gae Aulenti, Oriol Bohigas, Vittorio Gregotti, *Avanguardia e Professione*, in "Lotus International," no. 25, 1979.
Gae Aulenti, *Una geometria mentale*, in "Rassegna," no. 4, 1980.
Gae Aulenti, Franco Quadri, Luca Ronconi, *Il Laboratorio di Prato*, Ubulibri, Milan 1981.
Gae Aulenti, *Universum Theatri*, in "Casabella," no. 479, 1982.
Gae Aulenti, Italo Rota, *La corte dei Re*, in "Lotus International," no. 35, 1982.
Gae Aulenti, *Un punto di vista sull'ar-*

chitettura del teatro, in "Casabella," no. 502, 1984.
Gae Aulenti, Marco Vallora, *Quartetto della maledizione*, Ubulibri, Milan 1985.
Gae Aulenti, *Il giardiniere e il fotografo*, in Daniela Palazzoli (ed.), *Il secondo paradiso. La fotografia vista da Gae Aulenti. Natura e giardino nelle immagini dei grandi fotografi*, Fabbri Editori, Milan 1992.
Gae Aulenti, *Lavorare con la musica*, in "I Quaderni della Civica Scuola di Musica," no. 25, 1995 (Proceedings of the Conference "Music, Space, Architecture," Milan Triennale, 1994).
Gae Aulenti, *Programma architettonico-funzionale e Programma tecnico*, in AA.VV. *Il Castello di Milano. Una proposta di valorizzazione e rilancio*, Il Sole 24 Ore / Pirola, Milan 1995.
Gae Aulenti, *Opinioni e progetti*, in "Casabella," no. 630/631, 1996.
Gae Aulenti, *Il nuovo allestimento museale delle Scuderie del Quirinale*, in *Il Libro dell'anno 2000*, Ist. Enciclopedia Italiana Treccani, Rome 2001.

Articles on individual projects

Single family house with stable in San Siro, Milan, 1956
"Casabella," no. 219, 1958.

Single family villa in Camisasca, Como, 1959
"Casabella," no. 241, 1960.

Apartment in Via Turati, Milan, 1959
"Domus," no. 367, 1960. "Japan Interior Design," Sept. 1962. "Rassegna," no. 58, 1994.

House-studio in Via Cesariano, Milan, 1959
"Domus," no. 367, 1960. "Japan Interior Design," Sept. 1962.

12th MilanTriennale, Apartment in the city centre and Entrance to the Triennale from the Park, 1960
"Casabella," no. 243, 1960. "Rassegna," no. 10, 1982.

Rocking chair *Sgarsul*, 1962
"Domus," no. 395, 1962.

Holiday Center at the Tonale Pass, 1962
"Casabella," no. 276, 1963.

House in the wood, 1963
"Casabella," no. 291, 1964.

Furnishing for the Hotel Principe & Savoia, Milan, 1963
"Domus," no. 431, 1965.

13th Milan Triennale, Layout of Italian Section *Il tempo delle vacanze*, 1964
"Casabella," no. 290, 1964. "Domus," no. 417, 1964. "L'Oeil," no. 117, 1964. "Rassegna," no. 10, 1982.

Locus Solus furniture series, 1964
"Domus," no. 429, 1965.

Aprilina folding chair, 1964
"Domus," no. 706, 1989.

Max Mara offices and showroom, Milan, 1965
"Domus," no. 465, 1968.

Olivetti Showroom, Paris, 1967
"Domus," no. 452, 1967. "L'Oeil," no. 149, 1967. "L'Architecture d'Aujourd'hui," no. 188, 1976.

King Sun table lamp, 1967
"Domus," no. 456, 1967.

Olivetti Showroom in Buenos Aires, 1968
"Domus," no. 466, 1968. "L'Architecture d'Aujourd'hui," no. 188, 1976.

Dior shop in Parly 2, Paris, 1968
"L'Oeil," no. 181, 1970.

Knoll International Showroom, Boston, 1968
"L'Oeil," no. 201-202, 1971.

House for an Art Collector, Milan, 1969
"Domus," no. 482, 1970. "L'Oeil," no. 185, 1970. "Maison & Jardin," no. 169, 1971. "Rassegna," no. 58, 1994.

Apartment in Via Borgospesso, Milan, 1969
"Casa Vogue," no. 5, 1970.

House-studio in Via Annunciata, Milan, 1969
"Casa Vogue," no. 11, 1971.

Knoll International Showroom, New York, 1969
"Interiors," Aug. 1970. "L'Oeil," no. 201-202, 1971.

Apartment in Via Gabba, Milan, 1969
"Domus," no. 507, 1972. "House & Garden," June 1972. "Rassegna," no. 58, 1994.

Layout of Olivetti travelling exhibition *Concept and Form*, Paris, Barcelona, Madrid, Edinburgh, Tokyo, 1969-1970
"L'Oeil," no. 180, 1969. "Domus," no. 493, 1970. "Industrial Design," no. 17, 1970. "Design," no. 262, 1970. "L'Architecture d'Aujourd'hui," no. 188, 1976. "Rassegna," no. 10, 1982.

Garden in Tuscany, 1970
"House & Garden," Oct. 1971. "Domus," no. 499, 1971. "Casa Vogue," no. 13, 1972.
Gae Aulenti, *Un progetto mediterraneo*, in AA.VV., *Altri giardini altri orti*, Automobilia, Milan 1986.

FIAT Showroom, Brussels, 1970
"Domus," no. 528, 1973. "Ottagono," no. 35, 1974.

FIAT Showroom, Zurich, 1970
"Domus", no. 528, 1973. "Ottagono," no. 35, 1974.

Apartment with roof terrace, Florence, 1971
"Domus," no. 499, 1971.

Single family villa in Capalbio, Grosseto, 1971
"Lotus," no. 8, 1974.

International competition for the Business Center, Perugia, 1971
"Controspazio," no. 1-2, 1972.

House in Paraggi, 1971
"Casa Vogue," no. 41-42, 1975.

The Grotta Rosa, Amalfi, 1972
"Casa Vogue," no. 19, 1973. "House & Garden," March 1974.

Apartment at Torre del Grillo, Rome
"Connaissance des Arts," no. 261, 1973. "Casa Vogue," no. 33, 1974. "Maison Francaise", no. 297, 1976.

Participation in exhibition *Italy: The New Domestic Landscape* at the Museum of Modern Art, New York, 1972
"Casabella," no. 366, 1972. "Abitare," no. 107, 1972. "Domus," no. 510, 1972. "Ottagono," no. 25, 1972. "Rassegna," no. 58, 1994.

Project for "Milan instead of Milan," ADI International competition, 1972
"Casabella," no. 372, 1972.

Manual for the layout of FIAT showrooms, 1973
"Domus," no. 528, 1973.

Single family house in San Michele di Pagana, Genoa, 1973
"Global Interior," no. 8, 1974. "House & Garden," April 1977.

Villa "La Besozza," Paraggi, Genoa, 1973
"House & Garden," Sept. 1975.

Villa in Pisa, 1973
"Casa Vogue," no. 89, 1978. "Lotus," no. 22, 1979.

Neighborhood for 3500 inhabitants with Primary School and Middle School, Cinisello Balsamo, Milan, 1973
AA.VV., *Una nuova scuola di base. Esperienze di tempo pieno*, Emme Edizioni, Milan 1973.

House-studio in Piazza San Marco, 1974
"Casa Vogue," no. 46, 1975. *The House of the Architect*, edited by Anatxu Zabalbeascoa, Gustavo Gili, Barcelona 1995.

Apartment in Via Gesù, Milan, 1974
"Casa Vogue," no. 64, 1976.

Villa in Parma, 1975
"Lotus," no. 8, 1974. "Casa Vogue," no. 50, 1975. "Connaissance des Arts," no. 284, 1975. "AD Architectural Digest," no. 11-12, 1975. "Bolaffi Arte," no. 50, 1975.

Apartment in Via Tessa, Milan, 1976
"Casa Vogue," no. 83, 1978.

Furniture series for Knoll, 1976
"Domus," no. 584, 1978.

Theatre Planning Workshop, Prato, 1976-1978
"Lotus," no. 17, 1977.
Gae Aulenti, Franco Quadri, Luca Ronconi, *Il laboratorio di Prato*, Ubulibri, Milan 1981.

Stage design for *The Wild Duck* by Henrik Ibsen, 1977-1978
"Lotus," no. 17, 1977, "Ottagono," no. 47, 1977.

La Rosa House, Gubbio, 1978
"Casa Vogue," no. 158, 1984.

Single family house Gubbio, Perugia, 1978
"Casa Vogue," no. 191, 1987.

Consultation for Zone 2, Isola-Garibaldi-Porta Nuova, Milan, 1979
"Casabella," no. 451-452, 1979.

Musée d'Orsay, Paris, 1980-1986
"Casabella," no. 482, 1982. "Urbanistica," no. 81, 1985. "Domus," no. 679, 1987. "Connaissance des Arts," Musée d'Orsay ,1987. "Lotus," no. 53, 1987. *Gae Aulenti e il Museo d'Orsay*, Quaderni di Casabella, supplement to "Casabella," no. 535, 1987. "GA Global Architecture," no. 19, 1988.
Gae Aulenti, *Simulazione di progetto*, in "Corso di formazione alla professione di Architetto," Ordine degli Architetti della Provincia di Milano, 1994.

Stage design for *Donnerstag aus Licht* by Karlheinz Stockhausen, 1981
"Modo," no. 42, 1981.

Apartment in Via Santa Valeria, Milan, 1981
"Casa Vogue," no. 126, 1982.

Apartment in Piazza Castello, Milan, 1982
"Casa Vogue," no. 155, 1984.

Guest quarters and offices on Champs Elysées, Paris, 1982
"Casa Vogue," no. 180, 1986.

National Museum of Modern Art in Georges Pompidou Centre, Paris, 1982-1985
"Casabella," no. 515, 1985. "L'Architecture d'Aujourd'hui," no. 240, 1985. "Lotus," no. 53, 1987. "Anfione Zeto," no. 11, 1995.

Re-use of the Lingotto, Turin, 1983
AA.VV,. *Venti progetti per il futuro del Lingotto*, Etas Libri, Milan 1984.

Apartment in Via dei Pellegrini, Milan, 1983
"Casa Vogue," no. 155, 1984.

Apartment in Portofino, Genoa, 1983
"Casa Vogue," no. 187, 1987.

Participation in XVII Milan Triennale *Elective Affinities* with the project *The Harmonious Box. The Room of Mirrors*, 1985
"Casa Vogue," no. 160, 1985. "Domus," no. 660, 1985.

Stage design for *Rigoletto* by Giuseppe Verdi, *La Fanciulla del West* by Giacomo Puccini, *Cavalleria Rusticana* by Pietro Mascagni, *Pagliacci* by Ruggero Leoncavallo, Ravenna 1985
Gae Aulenti, Marco Vallora, *Quartetto della maledizione*, Ubulibri, Milan 1985.

Palazzo Grassi, Venice, 1985-1986
"Domus," no. 674, 1986. "Ottagono," no. 83, 1986. "Lotus," no. 53, 1987.

National Museum of Catalan Art in Palau Nacional de Montjuic, Barcelona, 1985-2004
"A&V Arquitectura y Vivienda," no. 16, 1988. "GA Global Architecture," no. 23, 1989. "Lotus," no. 83, 1994. "Domus," no. 784, 1996.

Bicocca Project, Milan, 1986
"Casabella," no. 524, 1986. AA.VV., *Progetto Bicocca*, Electa, Milan 1986.

"Adrienne Vittadini" stores, USA, 1987-1992
"House & Garden," July 1988. "Interior Design," Febr. 1989.

Stage design for *Zar Saltan* by Nikolaj Rimskij-Korsakov, 1988
"Domus," no. 700, 1988.

Marina B shop, Milan, 1989
"Casa Vogue," no. 216, 1990.

Villa in St. Tropez, 1990
"Casa Vogue," no. 232, 1991. "House Beautiful," Aug. 1993.

Entrance to Santa Maria Novella Station, Florence 1990
"Domus," no. 733, 1991. AA.VV., *Quinta Mostra Internazionale di Architettura*, La Biennale, Venice / Electa, Milan 1991. "Lotus," no. 74, 1992.

Italian Pavilion at EXPO '92, Seville, 1990-1992
"GA Global Architecture", no. 29, 1991. *Expo '92 Sevilla. Arquitectura y Diseno*, Electa, Milan 1992.

Layout for the exhibition *The Celts* at Palazzo Grassi, Venice, 1991
"Domus," no. 732, 1991. "Domus Dossier," no. 4, 1997, *Allestimenti*.

Remodelling of the Palazzo del Governo, Città di San Marino, 1991-1996
"Ottagono," no. 124, 1997.

Greater Istanbul Municipality Nejat F. Eczacibasi Art Museum, Istanbul, 1992
"GA Global Architecture," no. 36, 1993. "Lotus," no. 83, 1994.

International invited competition for the Sakuraokacho Hotel-Office Building, Tokyo 1992
"Arq," Università degli Studi di Napoli, no. 16, 1997.

International invited competition for the New Chaucery of the Italian Embassy, Washington D.C., 1992
"Casabella," no. 602, 1993.

Banner shop, Milan 1993
"Interior Design," Dec. 1993.

International invited competition for the Aragon Museum of Contemporary Art, Saragoza, 1993
"Lotus," no. 83, 1994.

Feasibility study for Sforza Castle, Milan 1993-1995
"Abitare," no. 323, 1993. AA.VV. *Il Castello di Milano. Una proposta di valorizzazione e rilancio*, Il Sole 24 Ore / Pirola, Milan 1995.

Temporary Exhibition Gallery at the Milan Triennale, 1994
"Casabella," no. 618, 1994. "Lotus," no. 83, 1994. "Domus," no. 767, 1995. "Anfione Zeto," no. 11, 1995.

Layout for the exhibition *The Italian Metamorphosis 1943-1968* at the Guggengeim Museum, New York, 1994
"Panorama," 1994/10/21. "Flash Art," no. 188, 1994. "Domus," no. 767, 1995. "Anfione Zeto," no. 11, 1995.

Layout for the exhibition *The Italian Metamorphosis 1943-1968* at the Kunstmuseum, Wolfsburg, 1995
"Anfione Zeto," no. 11, 1995.

Apartment in Paris, 1995
"Elle Décor," Aprile 1998.

Piazza in front of the former "Leopolda" station, Florence, 1996
"Abitare," no. 355, 1996.

New Asian Art Museum of San Francisco, 1996-2003
Guido Vergani, Gae Aulenti. *Una casa per l'Oriente*, in "La Stampa," 1996/12/9.
Federico Rampini, *San Francisco, città della frontiera. Gae Aulenti progetta il Museo Asiatico*, in "la Repubblica," 2000/11/4.
Zahid Sardar, *An Asian Reprise*, in "San Francisco Chronicle Magazine," 2001/5/20.
Jesse Hamlin, *Ascending into light and a world of art*, in "San Francisco Chronicle," 2002/3/10.

Salone dei Corazzieri at the Palazzo del Quirinale, Rome, 1997
"Bollettino d'Arte del Ministero per i Beni e le Attività Culturali," special volume on *Restoration work at the Quirinale*, no. 5, 1999.

International tender-competition for the reconstruction of La Fenice Theatre, Venice, 1997
"Lotus," no. 103, 1999.
I progetti per la ricostruzione del Teatro La Fenice, 1997, Marsilio Editori, Venice 2000.

International invited consultation for the new exit from the Uffizi in Piazza Castellani, Florence, 1998
La nuova uscita degli Uffizi. Progetti per piazza Castellani, Giunti, Florence 1998.

Spazio Oberdan, Milan, 1999
"Abitare," no. 375, 1998. "Lotus," no. 103, 1999.

Preliminary project for the new layout of the "piano nobile" of Palazzo del Quirinale, Rome, 1999
Gae Aulenti, *Il Quirinale. Progetto preliminare per il nuovo assetto del piano nobile*, Skira, Milan 1999.

Former Papal Stables at the Quirinale, Rome, 1999
Nino Criscenti, *Le Scuderie Papali al Quirinale. La nascita di un museo*, Agenzia Romana per la Preparazione del Giubileo, Rome 1999.
Gae Aulenti, *Il nuovo allestimento museale delle Scuderie del Quirinale*, in *Il Libro dell'anno 2000*, Ist. Enciclopedia Italiana Treccani, Rome 2001.

"Museo" and "Dante" Stations on Underground Line 1 and redesign of Piazza Cavour and Piazza Dante, Naples, 1999-2002
La Metropolitana di Napoli. Nuovi spazi per la mobilità e la cultura, Electa, Naples 2000.
"L'Industria delle Costruzioni," no. 360, 2001.

Piazzale Cadorna and the new façade of the Ferrovie Nord, Milan, 2000
"Abitare," no. 394, 2000. "Lotus," no. 106, 2000.

PHOTOGRAPHIC
CREDITS

Peppe Avallone for M.N. Metropolitana di Napoli 68 (bottom)
Aldo Ballo 48, 49, 204, 206, 207, 208, 211, 213 (top), 214, 216, 217, 219 (bottom)
Gabriele Basilico 38, 43, 44 (bottom), 45, 158
Elio Basso 202
Gianni Berengo Gardin 152-153
Osvaldo Böhm 159
Mario Carrieri 26-27, 30, 209
Valerio Castelli 224-225
Piero Castiglioni 54
Centrokappa 221
Giovanni Chiaramonte 166, 167
Mario Ciampi 168, 171
Carla De Benedetti 22-23, 24-25, 34-35, 37, 201
Tilde De Tullio and Federico Brandani 100, 101 (bottom), 190, 191, 192, 193
Ecoart 46, 47
Electa 55
Robert Emmett Bright 154, 155
Alberto Fioravanti/Colore Industriale 150
Vincenzo Antonio Greco 71
I Guzzini 57
Erich Hartmann/Magnum Photos 146-147

David Heald/The Solomon R.Guggenheim Foundation New York 162, 164, 165
Industrialfoto 140
Mimmo Jodice 31, 32, 33
Lelli & Masotti/Archivio Fotografico Teatro alla Scala 94, 95, 96-97, 101 (top), 102-103, 108, 109
Luciano Locatelli 104
Marco Marrè 65
Ugo Mulas 148, 149, 151
Marcello Norberth 84, 86 (bottom), 87, 89
Alberto Novelli 178, 180, 181
Nuova Arcadia cover, 50, 51, 52, 53, 90-91, 91, 94 (top)
Perretti & Park 59
Enzo Ragazzini 142-143, 240-241
RAI 105
RM 144-145, 200
Luciano Romano 106-107, 107
Guia Sambonet 174, 176, 177, 188, 189
Pietro Savorelli 129
Mia Serra 39, 42, 44 (top)
Enrico Sicignano 67, 68 (top)
Dario Tettamanzi 56
Carlo Valsecchi 186